Good Housekeeping

Brilliant
BAKING

When using kitchen appliances please always follow
the manufacturer's instructions.

HarperCollins*Publishers*
1 London Bridge Street
London SE1 9GF

www.harpercollins.co.uk

HarperCollins*Publishers*
1st Floor, Watermarque Building, Ringsend Road
Dublin 4, Ireland

First published by HarperCollins*Publishers* 2021

10 9 8 7 6 5 4 3 2 1

Project editor: Tracy Müller-King
Design by Louise Leffler

Recipe writers: Meike Beck, Emma Franklin, Alice Shields,
Georgie D'Arcy Coles, Grace Evans, Gabriella English, Suzannah
Butcher, Elisabeth Hutchinson, Madeleine Burkitt, Lucy Jessop,
Sophie Austen-Smith, Monaz Dumasia, Charlotte Watson, Zoë Horne,
Olivia Spurrell

Photographers: Kate Whitaker, Gareth Morgans, Alex Luck,
Kris Kirkham, Sam Stowell, Charlie Richards, Myles New, Will Heap,
Mike English, Steve Baxter, Maja Smend, Toby Scott, Simon Walton

A catalogue record of this book is available from the British Library

ISBN 978-0-00-839538-4

Printed and bound by GPS Group

MIX
Paper from
responsible sources
FSC™ C007454

FSC
www.fsc.org

Good Housekeeping

Brilliant BAKING

130 DELICIOUS RECIPES FROM BRITAIN'S MOST TRUSTED KITCHEN

HarperCollins*Publishers*

Contents

Foreword by Gaby Huddart, Editor-in-Chief

Could any smell be better than that of a freshly baked loaf emerging from the oven? Or any treat bigger than freshly made scones with jam and cream for afternoon tea? Or any taste more delicious than a birthday cake that someone has made for you knowing exactly what your taste buds enjoy? And is there anything more satisfying than passing round the biscuits or flapjacks that you've made and hearing the grateful 'mmms' of family and friends as they tuck in?

More than any other form of cooking, it's baking that has the ability to spread joy – both for the baker and for the recipient of their endeavours. Here's an activity that brings a little magic, creating nice, warm fuzzy feelings inside us, almost akin to a wonderful hug!

You don't need to be a psychologist to realise the power of this pastime. Just consider what happened during the various lockdowns of 2020 and 2021 when people right across the country found comfort in baking banana bread, and growing cultures in order to make sourdough became a craze. Conversations with friends and family over Zoom tended to focus either on discoveries of brilliant series on Netflix or sharing fabulous new recipes.

On our website, goodhousekeeping.com/uk, we marvelled as we saw millions logging on for troubleshooting articles on baking bread, easy three-ingredient bakes, and what to make when it was impossible to find eggs in the supermarket.

In my own home, I watched as my teenage daughter, Lara – until then a fan of watching *The Great British Bake Off* on TV from the comfort of an armchair – turned herself into the real deal, up at dawn (yes, dawn!) kneading and proving in order to be able to produce a wholemeal loaf in time for breakfast. As GCSEs were cancelled, revision was replaced with a hive of industry in the kitchen and Lara's cupcake creations also became an almost daily occurrence. She was just one of the many for whom baking became a kind of mindfulness therapy as the focus on following the recipes and the various processes involved took her mind off everything else and gave her a sense of calm and being in control, as well as creating something to be proud of (and, of course, to post on social media!).

And 'creating' is absolutely the right term for baking because, more than with other forms of cooking, there is definitely some alchemy at work. Something almost magical happens in the baker's kitchen, whereby some really simple ingredients are mixed together and become eminently greater than the sum of their parts. Eggs, flour, butter and sugar are mixed, put in the oven and a short time later rise into a beautifully light sponge. A little yeast is added to flour, salt, oil and water and, hey presto, a loaf is born!

In good times, tea and cake is an indulgence right at the heart of gatherings with friends, but even during our recent most bizarre of times, exchanging baked goods has been a way of showing others we care. Often when Lara baked, she left a tin with a slice of cake, a blueberry muffin or a few biscuits on the doorstep of our neighbour, who lives alone, and they never failed to raise his spirits and a smile even on the bleakest of lockdown days.

For many of us, there are fond memories deep within us that link baking with happy times and treasured people – think of blowing out candles on those early birthday cakes, or of afternoon tea spent with grandparents or, perhaps, of cutting a wedding cake. It's little wonder that

the old estate agent's adage about the smell of baking selling houses still rings true – one mere whiff is guaranteed to get those positive endorphins flowing!

So, with all of this in mind, we felt there was no better time than now to pull together our collection of favourite breads, cakes and bakes from the *Good Housekeeping* kitchens to give you all the inspiration you need for creating magic and memories – and simply to spread the joy of baking.

All of these bakes, under the incredible leadership of our cookery director Meike Beck and with the support of her wonderful team – Emma, Alice, Grace and Georgie – have been triple-tested to perfection so these are recipes that you can rely on to work every time. Our Tried, Tested, Trusted trademark is one that we take exceptionally seriously, so you can cook with confidence.

Not sure of where to start? Some of my own favourites include the recipes for Ultimate Brownies, Best-ever Carrot Cake, the Vegan Chocolate Cake and Alice's Marmalade and White Chocolate Loaf. That last bake is one of the most joyous creations I have ever tasted and proof that the results of baking are definitely greater than the sum of their parts.

Gaby

Dietary Information

Those following a vegetarian, vegan, gluten-free
or dairy-free diet will find recipes throughout
the cookbook where you see these symbols:

(VN) Vegan recipes

(GF) Gluten-free recipes

(DF) Dairy-free recipes

(V) Vegetarian recipes

- Check all packaging if following a specific
  diet, as brands vary.
- Not all cheese is vegetarian, although
  vegetarian cheeses (and dairy-free cheese
  suitable for a vegan diet) are widely
  available in supermarkets and health food
  stores. Always read the label and look out for
  the Vegetarian Society Approved symbol.
- Vegetable stock is not always vegan, and
  may contain gluten or dairy – always check
  the label if you are following a special diet.
- Wine may contain animal protein, so
  check the label to ensure it is suitable for
  vegetarians or vegans.

The Measurements

OVEN TEMPERATURES

°C	Fan Oven	Gas mark
110	90	¼
130	110	½
140	120	1
150	130	2
170	150	3
180	160	4
190	170	5
200	180	6
220	200	7
230	210	8
240	220	9

WEIGHTS

Metric	Imperial
15g	½oz
25g	1oz
40g	1½oz
50g	2oz
75g	3oz
100g	3½oz
125g	4oz
150g	5oz
175g	6oz
200g	7oz
225g	8oz
250g	9oz
275g	10oz
300g	11oz
350g	12oz
375g	13oz
400g	14oz
425g	15oz
450g	1lb
550g	1¼lb
700g	1½lb
900g	2lb
1.1kg	2½lb

VOLUMES

Metric	Imperial
5ml	1 tsp
15ml	1 tbsp
25ml	1fl oz
50ml	2fl oz
100ml	3½fl oz
125ml	4fl oz
150ml	5fl oz (¼ pint)
175ml	6fl oz
200ml	7fl oz
250ml	9fl oz
300ml	10fl oz (½ pint)
500ml	17fl oz
600ml	1 pint
900ml	1½ pints
1 litre	1¾ pints
2 litres	3½ pints

LENGTHS

Metric	Imperial
5mm	¼in
1cm	½in
2cm	¾in
2.5cm	1in
3cm	1¼in
4cm	1½in
5cm	2in
7.5cm	3in
10cm	4in
15cm	6in
18cm	7in
20.5cm	8in
23cm	9in
25.5cm	10in
28cm	11in
30.5cm	12in

ALWAYS REMEMBER

- Use one set of measurements – never mix metric and imperial.
- Ovens and grills must be preheated to the specified temperature before cooking.
- All spoon measures are for calibrated measuring spoons and should be level, unless otherwise stated.
- Eggs are medium and free-range and butter is salted, unless otherwise stated.
- Buy the best-quality meat you can afford.

1

Biscuits

Baci di Dama

These Italian biscuits (the name translates to 'Lady's Kisses') are often made with hazelnuts or almonds, but we've used pistachios here for a twist.

100g pistachios
100g butter, softened
100g caster sugar
100g plain flour

FOR THE FILLING
75g dark chocolate (70% cocoa solids), chopped

Hands-on time: 25min, plus chilling, cooling and setting
Cooking time: about 20min
Makes about 40 sandwiched biscuits

PER BISCUIT 63cals, 1g protein, 4g fat (2g saturates), 6g carbs (4g total sugars), trace fibre

◆ TO STORE
Keep in an airtight container at room temperature for up to a week.

1. Heat the oven to 180°C (160°C fan) mark 4. Scatter the pistachios on a small baking tray and toast in the oven for 5min. Set aside to cool.

2. Whizz the pistachios in a food processor until finely ground. Add the butter and sugar, and whizz until creamy. Add the flour and pulse until the dough clumps together, then tip on to a work surface and bring fully together with your hands. Wrap and chill for 1hr.

3. Line 2 large baking sheets with baking parchment. Pinch off 5g pieces of the chilled dough and roll into balls, then put on the lined baking sheets, spacing slightly apart. Chill again for 30min.

4. Reheat the oven to 180°C (160°C fan) mark 4 and bake the biscuits for 12–15min, or until lightly golden around the edges. Leave to cool completely on the trays.

5. For the filling, melt the chocolate in a heatproof bowl set over a pan of barely simmering water. Use the melted chocolate to sandwich together the bases of 2 cooled biscuits. Repeat until all the biscuits are sandwiched. Leave to set before serving.

Lemon and Cranberry Shortbreads

Using a food processor means these golden fingers are easy to make, and they're wonderful with a cup of tea.

200g unsalted butter, chilled and cubed
125g icing sugar
300g plain flour
2 tsp vanilla extract
50g dried cranberries, finely chopped
Finely grated zest 1 lemon

TO FINISH (optional)
150g white chocolate, chopped
Edible sprinkles

Hands-on time: 25min, plus chilling and cooling
Cooking time: about 50min
Makes about 22 biscuits

PER BISCUIT (with chocolate) 184cals, 2g protein, 10g fat (6g saturates), 22g carbs (11g total sugars), 1g fibre

◆ TO STORE
Keep cooled biscuits in an airtight container at room temperature for up to 5 days. If painted with chocolate, separate the biscuit layers with baking parchment.

1. Line a 20.5cm square tin with baking parchment and set aside. In a food processor, whizz the butter, sugar and flour with a pinch of salt until the mixture just clumps together. Add the vanilla, cranberries and lemon zest and pulse to combine.

2. Press the mixture into the prepared tin and level (using your hands or the back of a metal spoon is easiest). Prick the dough well with a fork, then chill for 30min.

3. Heat the oven to 170°C (150°C fan) mark 3. Bake the shortbread for 45–50min or until nicely golden.

4. While still warm, cut the shortbread in half across the middle, then cut each half into 1.5cm wide fingers. Cool completely in tin.

5. If finishing the biscuits with chocolate, line a baking sheet with baking parchment. Melt the chocolate in a heatproof bowl set over a pan of barely simmering water. Using a pastry brush, paint chocolate on one end of each shortbread finger, then arrange on the baking sheet. Decorate with sprinkles and leave to set, or chill for 15min.

Chocolate Honey Hearts

Warmly spiced with a dark chocolate coating, these cake-like treats are inspired by the classic Danish biscuits served at Christmas time.

250g runny honey
25g light brown muscovado sugar
300g self-raising flour, plus extra to dust
1 tsp ground cinnamon
½ tsp ground allspice
½ tsp ground cloves
1 medium egg yolk

TO DECORATE
200g dark chocolate (70% cocoa solids), chopped
Edible gold stars, to decorate (optional)

Hands-on time: 35min, plus cooling, overnight chilling and setting
Cooking time: about 14min
Makes 16 hearts

PER BISCUIT 186cals, 3g protein, 4g fat (2g saturates), 34g carbs (21g total sugars), 1g fibre

◆ TO STORE
Keep biscuits in an airtight container at room temperature for up to 5 days.

◆ GH TIP
For best results, temper your chocolate while melting it. This will stop it developing a white bloom (which is safe to eat but not as attractive). Melt 125g of your chocolate in a heatproof bowl set over a pan of simmering water and heat to 50°C. Take off the heat, stir in remaining 75g chocolate and allow to cool at room temperature to 31°C before using to coat your hearts.

1. Heat the honey and sugar together in a small pan to combine. Set aside to cool for 10min.

2. In a large bowl, mix the flour and spices, then add the honey mixture and egg yolk and stir to combine. Cover the bowl and chill for at least 6hr or ideally overnight to let the dough harden and the flavours develop.

3. Heat the oven to 180°C (160°C fan) mark 4. Line 2 large baking sheets with baking parchment. Tip the dough on to a lightly floured surface, bring together and roll out to 1cm thick. Stamp out 5cm wide hearts, re-rolling trimmings, and transfer to the prepared sheets. Space them 5cm apart as they will spread – you may need to bake them in batches.

4. Bake for 12-14min until sandy to the touch but still soft when pressed (they will harden slightly on cooling). Leave to cool on sheets for 10min before transferring to a wire rack to cool completely.

5. To decorate, melt the chocolate in a heatproof bowl set over a pan of simmering water (see GH TIP). Spoon over the biscuits (still on the rack) to cover. Sprinkle with gold stars, if you like, and leave to set.

Marbled Viennese Whirls

These two-tone, melt-in-the-mouth morsels will impress guests.

250g unsalted butter, very soft
50g icing sugar, sifted
1 tsp vanilla extract
250g plain flour
50g cornflour
1 tbsp cocoa powder

FOR THE FILLING
75g unsalted butter, softened
150g icing sugar, sifted
1 tbsp milk, room temperature
15g dark chocolate (at least 70% cocoa solids), grated

Hands-on time: 30min, plus chilling and cooling
Cooking time: about 15min
Makes about 17 sandwiched biscuits

PER BISCUIT 259cals, 2g protein, 16g fat (10g saturates), 26g carbs (13g total sugars), 1g fibre

◆ GET AHEAD
Keep sandwiched biscuits in an airtight container at room temperature for up to 3 days.

1. Heat the oven to 190°C (170°C fan) mark 5. In a medium bowl, beat together the butter, icing sugar and vanilla using a handheld electric whisk until light and very fluffy. Sift in the plain flour and cornflour and beat until just combined.

2. Split the mixture in half. Into one bowl, sift the cocoa powder and beat to combine. Line 2 large baking sheets with baking parchment.

3. Fill one side of a piping bag (fitted with a 1cm closed star nozzle) with the plain mixture, using your hands to shape it. Squash the chocolate mixture into the other side of the bag.

4. Pipe 2cm swirls on to the lined sheets, spacing them apart. The mixture will be very stiff – it helps if you seal the piping bag and squeeze from the middle rather than the top. Chill for 20min until firm. Bake for 15min until lightly golden. Cool on trays for a few minutes, then transfer to a wire rack to cool completely.

5. In a large bowl, beat together the butter, icing sugar and milk for the filling with a handheld electric whisk. Beat in the grated chocolate. Pipe or spread chocolate filling over the bases of half the biscuits, then sandwich together with the remaining biscuits and serve.

Florentines

Delicate, crisp and full of fruit and nuts, these are fun
to make and a joy to eat.

50g unsalted butter, chopped
75g demerara sugar
½ tbsp plain flour
1 tbsp double cream
40g dried cranberries, roughly chopped
25g chopped mixed peel
40g pistachios, roughly chopped
40g flaked almonds

TO DECORATE
100g dark or white chocolate, chopped, to taste

Hands-on time: 30min, plus cooling and setting
Cooking time: about 20min
Makes 12 biscuits

PER BISCUIT 168cals, 2g protein, 10g fat (4g
saturates), 16g carbs (14g total sugars), 1g fibre

◆ TO STORE
Keep in an airtight container at room temperature
for up to 5 days.

1. Heat the oven to 180°C (160°C fan) mark 4 and
   line 2 baking sheets with baking parchment.
   Heat the butter, sugar and flour in a heavy-based
   medium pan over low heat, stirring occasionally,
   until the sugar has nearly dissolved (it will look
   as if it's splitting, but will come together and
   start bubbling).

2. Take pan off heat and mix in the cream, followed
   by the dried fruit, mixed peel and nuts.

3. Dollop tablespoonfuls of mixture on to the
   prepared baking sheets, spacing them apart.
   Spread out each biscuit thinly and evenly.

4. Bake for 15min until golden, then allow to cool
   on the tray.

5. To finish, melt the chocolate in a heatproof
   bowl set over a pan of gently simmering water.
   Remove the bowl from the heat. Dip the base
   of each Florentine into the chocolate, then leave
   to set, chocolate-side up, on a cooling rack. If
   you want them to look authentic, run the tines
   of a fork in a wavy pattern over the chocolate
   when it's nearly set.

Home-made Wagon Wheels

Decadent and oh-so-good. If you don't have time to make the marshmallow filling, use a little Marshmallow Fluff spread instead.

175g plain flour, plus extra to dust
50g icing sugar
125g unsalted butter, chilled and chopped

FOR THE FILLING
1 medium egg white
3 tbsp caster sugar
½ tbsp golden syrup
75g raspberry jam

FOR THE COATING
175g dark chocolate (at least 70% cocoa solids), roughly
    chopped
175g milk chocolate, roughly chopped

Hands-on time: 45min, plus chilling and cooling
Cooking time: about 20min
Makes 8 sandwiched biscuits

PER BISCUIT 503cals, 5g protein, 26g fat (16g
saturates), 61g carbs (44g total sugars), 2g fibre

◆ TO STORE
Keep in an airtight container at room temperature
for up to 4 days.

1. For the biscuits, whizz the ingredients in a food
   processor until the mixture starts to clump
   together. Tip on to a work surface and knead
   to bring together. Shape into a disc, wrap in
   clingfilm and chill for 1hr.

2. Heat the oven to 180°C (160°C fan) mark 4
   and line 2 large baking sheets with baking
   parchment. Roll out the dough on a lightly
   floured surface until 3mm thick. Using an
   8cm round cutter, stamp out 16 circles,
   re-rolling trimmings as needed. Arrange
   on lined sheets (they don't spread much)
   and bake for 10–12min, or until sandy to the
   touch (they will firm up on cooling). Leave
   to cool completely on the sheets.

3. Meanwhile, make the marshmallow filling. In
   a large heatproof bowl set over a pan of barely
   simmering water, beat the egg white, sugar,
   golden syrup and a pinch of salt with a handheld
   electric whisk until the mixture has doubled
   in size and is the consistency of stiffly whipped
   double cream – this will take about 8min.
   Transfer to a piping bag (either fitted with
   a 5mm nozzle or you can snip a hole in the
   bag later) and set aside.

4. To assemble, cut out 8 x 8cm circles of baking
   parchment (draw around your biscuit cutter
   for ease) and arrange them on a wire rack set
   over a baking tray. Next, melt the chocolates
   in a heatproof bowl set over a pan of barely
   simmering water. Set aside to cool slightly.
   Spread a thin layer of raspberry jam over the
   top of 8 of the biscuits. Snip a 5mm hole in
   the end of your piping bag, if needed, and pipe
   a spiral of marshmallow filling over the jam
   on each base, to cover. Top with the remaining
   biscuits to create 8 sandwiches. Smooth the
   sides with a small palette knife, if needed.

5. Dunk the base of each sandwich into the melted
   chocolate, then place each on a parchment
   circle. Transfer the remaining chocolate to
   a jug and pour over the sandwiched biscuits,
   using a palette knife to ensure all sides are
   evenly coated. Chill in fridge to set. Peel the
   baking parchment off the base before serving.

Fig, Walnut and Parmesan Biscotti

A delectable savoury twist on a classic Italian biscuit.
Lovely with a glass of wine.

200g plain flour
1 tsp baking powder
100g Parmesan, finely grated
100g dried figs, chopped
75g walnuts, roughly chopped
Handful thyme sprigs, leaves picked
3 large eggs, beaten

Hands-on time: 20min, plus cooling
Cooking time: 1hr 15min
Makes about 32 biscotti

PER BISCOTTI 67cals, 3g protein, 3g fat (1g saturates),
6g carbs (2g total sugars), 1g fibre

◆ TO STORE
Keep in an airtight container at room temperature
for up to 2 weeks.

1. Heat the oven to 170°C (150°C fan) mark 3. Line
   2 large baking sheets with baking parchment
   In a bowl, mix the flour, baking powder,
   Parmesan, figs, walnuts, thyme leaves and
   1tsp each salt and freshly ground black pepper.
   Add the eggs and stir to form a soft dough.

2. Halve the dough and shape into two logs,
   each 25.5cm long by 6.5cm wide. Put one on
   each baking sheet and cook for 25min, until
   lightly golden.

3. Transfer to a wire rack to cool for 5min.
   Using a large serrated knife, cut across the
   logs, slicing each into 16.

4. Return the slices to the lined baking sheets,
   cut side up. Cook for 50min, flipping halfway.
   Transfer to a wire rack and cool completely.

Manchego and Thyme Shortbreads

Crumbly, buttery and delicately cheesy, these shortbreads are delicious by themselves, but also work well on a cheeseboard.

125g unsalted butter, softened
150g Manchego, or similar hard cheese, coarsely grated
1 medium egg yolk
1 tbsp thyme leaves
200g plain flour

Hands-on time: 20min, plus chilling and cooling
Cooking time: about 20min
Makes 24 biscuits

PER BISCUIT 101cals, 3g protein, 7g fat (5g saturates), 7g carbs (0g total sugars), trace fibre

◆ TO STORE
Keep in an airtight container at room temperature for up to 2 weeks.

1. In a large bowl, beat the butter, cheese, ½ tsp fine salt and 1 tsp freshly ground black pepper using a handheld electric whisk until light and creamy. Beat in the egg yolk and thyme leaves, followed by the flour, mixing just until the dough clumps together.

2. Tip on to a work surface and shape into a 5.5cm wide cylinder, making sure the ends are flat. Wrap in baking parchment or clingfilm and chill for 1½hr.

3. Heat the oven to 170°C (150°C fan) mark 3 and line 2 baking sheets with baking parchment. Slice the chilled dough into 5mm discs and space apart on the lined sheets. Bake for 20min, until golden. Leave to cool for a few minutes on the trays before transferring to a wire rack to cool completely.

Alfajores

These melt-in-the-mouth biscuits hail from South America. The addition of cornflour gives them a soft, crumbly texture.

125g unsalted butter, softened
100g caster sugar
2 large egg yolks
Finely grated zest 1 lemon
1 tsp vanilla bean paste
150g plain flour, plus extra to dust
100g cornflour
1 tsp baking powder
200g dulce de leche (see GH TIP)
25g desiccated coconut

Hands-on time: 25min, plus chilling
Cooking time: about 10min
Makes about 18 cookies

PER BISCUIT 209cals, 4g protein, 11g fat (6g saturates), 23g carbs (12g total sugars), 1g fibre

◆ GH TIP
If you can't find dulce de leche, use Carnation Caramel, jam or chocolate spread instead.

1. Using a freestanding mixer fitted with a paddle attachment (or a handheld electric whisk), beat the butter and sugar until pale and fluffy. Beat in the egg yolks one at a time, followed by the lemon zest and vanilla. Sift over the flours and baking powder, then mix to combine. Bring the dough together with your hands, wrap in clingfilm and chill for 1hr (or up to 24hr).

2. Line 2 large baking trays with baking parchment. Lightly dust a work surface with flour and roll out the dough until 3mm thick. Use a 5cm round cutter to stamp out circles, re-rolling trimmings as needed. Transfer to baking trays, spacing well apart. Chill for 10min.

3. Heat the oven to 180°C (160°C fan) mark 4. Bake the cookies for 8min, or until just set. Leave to cool on trays for 10min before transferring to a wire rack to cool completely.

4. Sandwich the biscuits together with dulce de leche, then roll the sides in coconut.

Gingernuts

One taste of these home-made classics and you'll
be hooked.

50g butter, chopped, plus extra to grease
125g self-raising flour, plus extra to dust
½ tsp bicarbonate of soda
2 tsp ground ginger
1 tsp ground cinnamon
2 tsp caster sugar
75g golden syrup

Hands-on time: 15min, plus cooling
Cooking time: about 12min
Makes 14 biscuits

**PER BISCUIT 78cals, 1g protein, 3g fat (2g saturates),
12g carbs (5g total sugars), trace fibre**

◆ TO STORE
Keep in an airtight container for up to a week.

1. Heat the oven to 190°C (170°C fan) mark 5.
   Lightly grease 2 baking sheets. Sift the flour,
   bicarbonate of soda, ginger and cinnamon into
   a large bowl. Mix in the sugar, then set aside.

2. Put the butter in a small pan and add the syrup.
   Heat gently until the butter has melted, then
   pour the mixture into the dry ingredients,
   stirring well.

3. Divide the dough into 14 equal pieces and roll
   each into a ball. Space them apart on the greased
   sheets and flatten them a little.

4. Bake for 12min. Cool slightly on the sheets, then
   transfer to a wire rack to cool completely.

Chocolate Oaties

These oatmeal biscuits dipped in chocolate will be a favourite with the whole family.

125g butter, plus extra to grease
125g self-raising flour
125g light brown soft sugar
125g porridge oats
½ tsp bicarbonate of soda
1 tbsp golden syrup
125g milk or dark (70% cocoa solids) chocolate, melted

Hands-on time: 30min, plus cooling and setting
Cooking time: about 20min
Makes 16 biscuits

PER BISCUIT 192cals, 2g protein, 10g fat (6g saturates), 24g carbs (13g total sugars), 1g fibre

◆ TO STORE
Keep the biscuits in an airtight container for up to a week.

1. Heat the oven to 180°C (160°C fan) mark 4 and lightly grease 2 baking sheets. In a large bowl, mix together the flour, sugar, oats and bicarbonate of soda. Set aside.

2. In a small pan, melt the butter and golden syrup. Add to the dry mixture and combine.

3. Divide the mixture into 16 and form into balls. Arrange on the baking sheets, spacing apart, and squash down a little. Bake for 15–18min until golden. Leave to cool for 3min on the trays, then transfer to a wire rack to cool completely.

4. Melt the chocolate in a heatproof bowl set over a pan of barely simmering water (or microwave on full power in a glass bowl for 20sec bursts until melted). Using a pastry brush, paint half of each biscuit (top and bottom), with chocolate. Alternatively, drizzle the chocolate liberally over the biscuits. Transfer biscuits to a wire rack to set before serving.

Bourbons

These addictive biscuits are easy to master – and well
worth the effort!

V

250g plain flour, plus extra to dust
125g unsalted butter, chilled, cut into cubes
125g caster sugar
2 tbsp golden syrup
50g cocoa powder
1 tsp bicarbonate of soda
3 tbsp milk

FOR THE FILLING
75g unsalted butter, softened
125g icing sugar
15g cocoa powder

Hands-on time: 30min, plus chilling and cooling
Cooking time: about 25min
Makes 18 biscuits

PER BISCUIT 206cals, 2g protein, 10g fat (7g
saturates), 28g carbs (17g total sugars), 1g fibre

◆ TO STORE
Keep in an airtight container for up to 5 days.

1. Heat the oven to 180°C (160°C fan) mark 4.
   Put all the biscuit ingredients into a food
   processor and pulse until the mixture clumps
   together. Tip the dough on to a work surface
   and bring it together with your hands.

2. Roll out the dough on a sheet of baking
   parchment, trying to keep it rectangular and
   dusting your rolling pin with flour as needed.
   Trim to a 23cm x 30.5cm rectangle. Cut the
   rectangle lengthways into 3 even strips, keeping
   the strips together, then cut across them at
   2.5cm intervals, keeping the rectangles together.
   If you like, use the end of a skewer to mark
   the long edges of each biscuit with five dots to
   resemble a traditional Bourbon. Chill for 30min.

3. Bake for 25min, then carefully remove the tray
   from the oven and cut through the marks to
   make sure the biscuits are separated. Leave
   to cool completely.

4. To make the filling, put the butter into a large
   bowl and sift in the icing sugar and cocoa
   powder. Mix until combined (don't be tempted
   to add any liquid – the icing should be thick).

5. Sandwich the cooled biscuits together with the
   chocolate filling, using a piping bag if you want
   a neater finish.

Ultimate Macarons

These French delights are notoriously tricky to make, but this easy-to-follow recipe will help you master the technique.

200g ground almonds
225g icing sugar
150g egg whites (3–4 eggs)
70g granulated sugar
1 tsp vanilla bean paste (optional)
Flavouring and colouring of your choice

FOR THE BUTTERCREAM
150g unsalted butter, softened
250g icing sugar, sifted
1 tbsp milk
Flavouring (optional)

Hands-on time: 1hr 15min
Cooking time: about 18min
30 servings

PER MACARON 155cals, 2g protein, 8g fat (3g saturates), 19g carbs (18g total sugars), 1g fibre

◆ GH TIPS
● Experiment with different ground nuts as a base – hazelnuts work well.
● You can use a handheld electric whisk to beat the egg whites – your macarons will still be shiny and delicious, but the frill at the bottom won't be as defined.
● For colour, use food colouring gels or pastes rather than liquids. Extracts and essences are the easiest way to add flavour.
● Flavour buttercream with extracts, essences, melted chocolate, chopped nuts, alcohol, etc. Dye it with food colouring gels or pastes.
● If your macarons crack when baked, it means you didn't release air bubbles when banging the tray on the work surface.
● Macarons keep covered in the fridge for up to 1 week.

1. Heat the oven to 170°C (150°C fan) mark 3. Line 2 large baking sheets with baking parchment. Draw 4cm circles on the parchment, spacing them about 2.5cm apart. Flip the parchment so the ink is underneath.

2. Work the ground almonds through a fine sieve until you have 115g, then sift over the icing sugar and a pinch of salt. Set aside. In a freestanding electric mixer, beat the egg whites, granulated sugar and vanilla bean paste (if using) at medium speed for 3min. Increase to medium-high for 3min, then turn up to maximum for 3min. Add any flavour or colour (see GH TIPS). Beat at full speed for 1min more.

3. Add the almond mixture in one go and use a silicone spatula to fold together, counting the folds – be firm, the aim is to knock the air out of the whites. After about 40 folds, it should move like lava. Transfer half the mix to a piping bag with a 1cm plain nozzle and pipe it inside the drawn circles. Repeat with the remaining mixture.

4. Bang the baking trays down hard against your counter a few times to burst any bubbles, then bake for 18min or until you can peel macarons from the paper. Allow to cool completely on the trays.

5. To make the buttercream, beat together the butter, icing sugar, milk and any flavouring until combined (see GH TIPS). Use to sandwich together the macaron, piping for a neat finish.

2

Loaf Cakes & Traybakes

Sticky Toffee Pudding Cake

This rich cake doubles as a comforting pudding, served with vanilla ice cream. The drizzle makes it extra gooey and delicious.

FOR THE CAKE
150g pitted Medjool dates, finely chopped
1 tsp bicarbonate of soda
100g unsalted butter, softened, plus extra to grease
75g light brown soft sugar
2 tbsp black treacle
2 medium eggs
150g self-raising flour (see GH TIP)
1 tsp baking powder

FOR THE DRIZZLE
50g unsalted butter
50g light brown soft sugar
1 tbsp black treacle
75ml double cream

Hands-on time: 20min, plus soaking and cooling
Cooking time: about 50min
Serves 8

PER SERVING 398cals, 4g protein, 22g fat (13g saturates), 45g carbs (30g total sugars), 2g fibre

◆ GH TIP
Avoiding gluten? Use gluten-free self-raising flour and check your brands of baking powder and bicarbonate of soda are gluten free.

◆ TO STORE
Keep in an airtight container in the fridge for up to 3 days. Allow to come to room temperature before serving.

1. Heat the oven to 180°C (160°C fan) mark 4. For the cake, put the dates and bicarbonate of soda into a small heatproof bowl and pour in 150ml just-boiled water. Leave to soak for 10min. Grease and line a 900g loaf tin with baking parchment.

2. In a large bowl, beat the butter and sugar using a handheld electric whisk until light and fluffy, about 5min. Beat in the black treacle, followed by the eggs, flour, baking powder and date mixture until just combined. Pour the mixture into the lined tin.

3. Bake for 40–50min, or until a skewer inserted in the centre comes out clean. Cool in the tin for 5min, then transfer to a wire rack to cool further.

4. Meanwhile, make the drizzle. Heat all the ingredients in a small pan over a low heat, stirring until the sugar dissolves. Bring to the boil and bubble for 2min, stirring constantly. Remove from the heat and leave to cool for 5min to thicken slightly, stirring occasionally to prevent it from splitting.

5. Serve the cake just warm or at room temperature topped with the drizzle.

Persian Tea Loaf

If you're not a fan of rosewater, use orange blossom water instead for this fragrantly exotic confection.

275ml hot, strong Earl Grey or English Breakfast tea
125g each dried figs and apricots, roughly chopped
150g sultanas
125g light brown soft sugar
10 green cardamom pods
75g pistachios, finely ground
200g self-raising flour
½ tsp rosewater
2 medium eggs, beaten

FOR THE ICING
150g icing sugar
Pink food colouring (optional)
25g pistachios, chopped
Dried rose petals (optional)

**Hands-on time: 30min, plus overnight soaking
   and cooling**
Cooking time: about 1hr 30min
Cuts into 10 slices

PER SLICE 349cals, 7g protein, 7g fat (1g saturates),
62g carbs (48g total sugars), 4g fibre

◆ TO STORE
Keep in an airtight container at room temperature
for up to a week.

1. Pour the tea into a medium bowl, then add the dried fruit and brown sugar. Stir to dissolve the sugar, then leave to soak for a minimum of 1hr or preferably overnight.

2. Heat the oven to 150°C (130°C fan) mark 2. Line a 900g loaf tin with baking parchment. Bash open the cardamom pods in a pestle and mortar, pick out the seeds and discard the husks. Grind the seeds to a powder, then scrape the ground cardamom into a large bowl and mix in the ground pistachios and flour. Add the soaked fruit mixture, rosewater and eggs and mix to combine.

3. Scrape the mixture into the prepared tin, level and bake for 1hr 20–1hr 30min until a skewer inserted into the centre comes out clean. Cool in the tin for 5min, then remove from the tin and cool completely in its parchment on a wire rack.

4. Transfer the cooled loaf to a board and remove the parchment. Sift the icing sugar into a bowl and mix in about 1½ tbsp cold water to make a thick but spreadable consistency (you may need a drop more water). Dye the icing pink with food colouring, if using, then spread it over the top of the cake so it dribbles down the sides. Scatter over pistachios and rose petals, if using. Allow to set before serving in slices.

Marbled Chai and Chocolate Loaf

This wonderfully spiced cake is topped with a decadent cream-cheese icing, but is just as delicious without it.

FOR THE CAKE
225g unsalted butter, softened, plus extra to grease
225g light brown soft sugar
275g self-raising flour
2 tsp baking powder
3 medium eggs
125g soured cream
2 tbsp cocoa powder, sifted

FOR THE CHAI MIXTURE
4 cardamom pods
½ tsp ground cinnamon
⅛ tsp ground cloves
½ tsp ground ginger
¼ tsp ground allspice

FOR THE ICING
50g unsalted butter, softened
100g full-fat cream cheese, at room temperature
200g icing sugar, sifted

Hands-on time: 20min, plus cooling
Cooking time: about 1hr
Cuts into 8 slices

PER SLICE 598cals, 8g protein, 27g fat (16g saturates), 80g carbs (53g total sugars), 2g fibre

◆ TO STORE
Keep in an airtight container in the fridge for up to 5 days. Allow to come to room temperature before serving.

1. Heat the oven to 180°C (160°C fan) mark 4 and lightly grease and line a 900g loaf tin with baking parchment. For the chai mixture, bash the cardamom pods using a pestle and mortar to break the husks. Pick out the black seeds, discard the husks and grind the seeds until fine. Mix in the remaining chai mix ingredients. Set aside.

2. For the cake, in a large bowl beat the butter, sugar, flour, baking powder, eggs and soured cream using a handheld electric whisk until light and fluffy, about 2min. Spoon half the mixture into a separate bowl and beat in most of the chai mixture (reserve some to decorate).

3. Sift the cocoa powder into the other cake batter bowl and beat to combine. Dollop alternate spoonfuls of the cake batters into the lined tin, lightly swirl together with a skewer or cutlery knife, then smooth to level.

4. Bake for 1hr, or until risen and a skewer inserted into the centre comes out clean. Cool the cake in the tin for 5min, then transfer to a wire rack to cool completely.

5. To make the icing, beat together all the ingredients using a handheld electric whisk until combined and fluffy. Pipe or spread over the top of the cooled cake and sprinkle over the remaining chai mixture. Serve in slices.

Chocolate Orange Cake

If you don't have time to make the topping, you could decorate this cake with Terry's Chocolate Orange segments instead.

FOR THE CAKE
200g unsalted butter, softened, plus extra to grease
200g caster sugar
3 medium eggs
125ml soured cream
275g self-raising flour
½ tsp baking powder
Finely grated zest 2 oranges, plus 1 tbsp juice
2 tbsp cocoa powder

FOR THE TOPPING
1 orange
125g dark chocolate, finely chopped
75g milk chocolate, finely chopped
75ml double cream

Hands-on time: 30min, plus cooling
Cooking time: about 1hr 10min
Serves 8

PER SERVING 444cals, 6g protein, 26g fat (16g saturates), 46g carbs (28g total sugars), 2g fibre

◆ TO STORE
Keep in airtight container in the fridge for up to 3 days. Allow to come to room temperature before serving.

1. Heat the oven to 180°C (160°C fan) mark 4 and lightly grease and line a 900g loaf tin with baking parchment. In a large bowl, beat the butter, sugar, eggs, soured cream, flour and baking powder using a handheld electric whisk until light and fluffy, about 3min. Spoon two-thirds of the mixture into a separate bowl and beat in the orange zest and juice.

2. In a separate small bowl, mix the cocoa powder and 2 tbsp just-boiled water to make a paste. Add this to the plain cake batter bowl and beat together to combine.

3. Dollop alternate spoonfuls of the 2 cake batters into the lined tin, then lightly swirl together with a skewer or cutlery knife to marble. Smooth to level. Bake for 1hr, or until risen and a skewer inserted into the centre comes out clean. Leave to cool completely in the tin.

4. For the topping, slice the top and bottom off the orange and sit on a board. Cut away the peel and white pith, then carefully cut between the membranes to separate the segments. Pat the segments dry with kitchen paper and set aside. Mix the 2 chocolates, then melt half the mixture in a heatproof bowl set over a pan of barely simmering water. Leave to cool slightly. Line a baking sheet with baking parchment. Dip half of each dried orange segment into the melted chocolate, lay on the lined sheet and leave to harden.

5. Put the remaining chopped chocolate into a clean heatproof bowl. Heat the cream in a small pan until hot. Pour into the chocolate bowl and stir until melted and smooth, then leave to firm up a bit. Transfer the cake to a board. Spread over the topping and lay on the dipped orange segments. Serve in slices.

Blueberry and Lemon Loaf Cake

Soured cream adds richness and helps to keep this cake deliciously moist.

50ml vegetable oil, plus extra to grease
200g self-raising flour
175g caster sugar
2 medium eggs
200g soured cream
2 tsp vanilla extract
Finely grated zest 2 lemons
125g blueberries

FOR THE ICING
75g icing sugar, sifted
1½ tbsp lemon juice

TO DECORATE (optional)
50g blueberries
Pared lemon zest
Edible flowers

Hands-on time: 15min, plus cooling
Cooking time: about 1hr 10min
Cuts into 8 slices

PER SLICE 347cals, 5g protein, 13g fat (4g saturates), 53g carbs (34g total sugars), 1g fibre

◆ GET AHEAD
This cake will keep for up to 3 days in an airtight container at room temperature.

1. Heat the oven to 180°C (160°C fan) mark 4. Grease and line a 900g loaf tin with baking parchment. In a large bowl, stir together the flour, sugar and a pinch of fine salt to combine. Add the remaining ingredients, except for the blueberries, and whisk briefly until just combined (a few lumps are a good thing in this recipe).

2. Fold in 100g of the blueberries and scrape the mixture into the prepared tin. Scatter over the remaining berries. Bake for about 1hr–1hr 10min, or until golden and a skewer inserted into the centre comes out clean. Cool in then tin for 10min, then gently ease out and leave to cool on a wire rack.

3. Mix the icing ingredients in a small bowl until smooth, then drizzle over the cooled cake. Scatter over the blueberries, lemon zest and edible flowers, if you like. Serve in slices.

Coconut and Raspberry Loaf

A classic combination that is topped with a billowy icing.

175g unsalted butter, softened, plus extra to grease
50g desiccated coconut
175g caster sugar
3 medium eggs, beaten
175g self-raising flour
150g raspberries

TO DECORATE
15g coconut flakes
1 medium egg white
175g caster sugar
Pinch cream of tartar
1 tsp Malibu (optional)
Freeze-dried raspberries, ground (optional)

Hands-on time: 30min, plus cooling
Cooking time: about 1hr 15min
Cuts into 10 slices

PER SLICE 404cals, 5g protein, 20g fat (13g saturates),
49g carbs (37g total sugars), 3g fibree

◆ TO STORE
The un-iced cake will keep in an airtight container
at room temperature for up to 1 week. Once iced,
eat within a day (as the icing becomes granular).

1. Heat the oven to 180°C (160°C fan) mark 4.
   Grease and line the base and sides of a 900g
   loaf tin with baking parchment. Spread the
   desiccated coconut thinly on a baking sheet,
   then cook in the oven for 2min or until very
   lightly toasted (it can burn quickly). Empty
   into a bowl and set aside.

2. In a large bowl, beat the butter and sugar with
   a handheld electric whisk until light and fluffy
   – about 5min. Add the eggs, beating well after
   each addition.

3. Fold in the flour and toasted coconut, then gently
   fold in the raspberries. Spoon into the prepared
   tin and spread to level. Bake for 55–65min, or
   until a skewer inserted into the centre comes out
   clean. Cool in tin for 10min, then remove from
   the tin and cool in its parchment on a wire rack.

4. Meanwhile, spread the coconut flakes on a
   baking sheet and cook in the oven for 2min,
   or until lightly toasted. Set aside.

5. Transfer the cooled loaf to a board and remove
   the parchment. For the icing, put the egg white,
   sugar, cream of tartar, a pinch of salt and 2 tbsp
   water into a heatproof bowl and beat with a
   handheld electric whisk. Put the bowl over a pan
   of simmering water and keep whisking until the
   mixture is thick and the sugar has all dissolved
   (9–10min). Whisk in the Malibu, if using, then
   spread the icing quickly over the cake. Sprinkle
   over the toasted coconut flakes and freeze-dried
   raspberries, if using. Serve in slices.

Ultimate Brownies

Looking for the perfect brownie that's glossy on top, dense and fudgy in the centre? Well, here it is…

175g unsalted butter, chopped, plus extra to grease
150g dark chocolate (70% cocoa solids), chopped
3 medium eggs
300g caster sugar
75g plain flour
40g cocoa powder
Icing sugar, to dust (optional)

Hands-on time: 20min, plus cooling
Cooking time: about 35min
Cuts into 16 squares

PER SQUARE 244cals, 3g protein, 13g fat
(8g saturates), 28g carbs (25g sugars), 1g fibre

◆ TO STORE
Keep well wrapped in foil or an airtight container
at room temperature for up to a week.

◆ GH TIP
Add a handful of your favourite chopped nuts
or plain/milk/white chocolate chunks for extra
crunch and decadence.

1. Melt the butter and chocolate together in a heatproof bowl set over a pan of barely simmering water (make sure the base of the bowl doesn't touch the water). When the mixture is melted and smooth, lift the bowl off the pan and set aside to cool for 30min.

2. Heat the oven to 180°C (160°C fan) mark 4 and lightly grease and line a 20.5cm square tin with baking parchment. Using a handheld electric whisk, beat the eggs and sugar together in a large bowl until the mixture is thick and moussey – about 5min.

3. Add the melted and cooled chocolate mixture to the egg bowl and fold together with a large metal spoon. Sift over the flour, cocoa powder and a pinch of salt and fold together.

4. Scrape the mixture into the prepared tin, level and bake for 30min or until there is no wobble left when you gently shake the tin. Cool completely in the tin before dusting with icing sugar (if you like) and cutting into squares.

Chocolate, Frangipane and Pear Tart

We've used tinned pears for this pretty tart, as they keep their colour better.

(V)

FOR THE PASTRY
200g plain flour, plus extra to dust
25g cocoa powder
40g caster sugar
175g unsalted butter, chilled

FOR THE CRUMBLE TOPPING
25g unsalted butter
25g flaked almonds
25g light brown soft sugar
25g plain flour

FOR THE FRANGIPANE FILLING
175g unsalted butter, softened
175g caster sugar
3 large eggs, beaten
50g plain flour
175g ground almonds
Few drops almond extract
8 tinned pear halves in juice, drained

Hands-on time: 40min, plus chilling and cooling
Cooking time: about 1hr 15min
Serves 8

PER SERVING 793cals, 14g protein, 56g fat (27g saturates), 57g carbs (32g total sugars), 5g fibre

◆ TO STORE
Keep in an airtight container at room temperature for up to 1 day.

1. To make the pastry, pulse the flour, cocoa powder, caster sugar and butter in a food processor until the mixture resembles fine breadcrumbs. Alternatively, rub the butter into the flour mixture using your fingertips. Add 3 tbsp cold water and pulse/mix until just coming together. Empty on to a work surface and briefly knead to bring together. Shape into a disc, wrap in clingfilm and chill for 30min.

2. To make the crumble topping, melt the butter in a small frying pan and add the remaining ingredients. Fry, stirring occasionally, for 3–4min until golden and toasted. Empty into a bowl and leave to cool.

3. Lightly flour a work surface and roll out the pastry. Use to line a 30.5 x 19cm rectangular tin, leaving some pastry overhanging the edges. Chill for 30min.

4. To make the frangipane, beat the butter and sugar together using a handheld electric whisk for 5min, until light and creamy. Gradually beat in the eggs. Fold in the flour, ground almonds and almond extract and set aside.

5. Heat the oven to 200°C (180°C fan) mark 6. Line the pastry with a large sheet of baking parchment. Fill with baking beans or uncooked rice. Bake for 15min until the pastry sides are set, then carefully remove the parchment and beans/ rice. Cook for a further 5min, until the pastry base feels sandy to the touch. Carefully remove from the oven and trim the edges with a serrated knife. Set aside to cool for 10min and lower the oven temperature to 160°C (140°C fan) mark 3.

6. Spoon the frangipane into the pastry case and smooth to level. Lay the pears on top, cut-side down. Sprinkle over the crumble topping and bake for 50min, until the frangipane is set and lightly golden. Leave to cool completely in the tin before transferring to a serving plate or board to slice.

Orange and Lemon Traybake

This recipe contains no butter or oil in the batter – all its richness comes from cooked, whole oranges.

Oil, to grease
2 oranges, skins washed
6 large eggs
225g caster sugar
1 tbsp vanilla extract
Grated zest 1 lemon
Grated zest 1 lime
1 tsp gluten-free baking powder
½ tsp freshly grated nutmeg
225g ground almonds

FOR THE SYRUP
Juice 1 orange
25g caster sugar

FOR THE ICING
1 tbsp flaked almonds, to decorate
75g icing sugar, sifted
1 tbsp freshly squeezed orange juice

Hands-on time: 25min, plus cooling
Cooking time: about 1hr 45min
Cuts into 12 squares

PER SQUARE 295cals, 9g protein, 14g fat (2g saturates), 31g carbs (31g total sugars), 2g fibre

◆ TO STORE
Keep the iced cake in an airtight container in a cool place for up to 5 days.

1. Grease a 30.5 x 23cm tin and line with baking parchment. Bring a large pan of water to the boil, add the oranges, then cover and boil for 1hr. Remove from the water and allow to cool.

2. Heat the oven to 180°C (160°C fan) mark 4. Once the oranges are cool enough to handle, cut in half and remove the pips. Put the fruit, including the skin, in a blender or food processor and blitz until smooth.

3. In a large bowl, beat the eggs and sugar together with a handheld electric whisk until pale and thick. Fold in the vanilla extract, lemon and lime zest, baking powder, nutmeg and ground almonds until incorporated. Fold through the puréed orange and combine well.

4. Pour the mixture into the prepared tin and bake for 35–40min until a skewer inserted comes out clean.

5. Meanwhile, make the syrup by gently heating the orange juice and sugar together in a pan over a medium heat.

6. Using a skewer, make holes in the warm cake and brush over the syrup so that it soaks in. Leave to cool completely.

7. In a small dry frying pan, toast the almonds over a medium heat for 3–5min. Remove from the heat. In a small bowl, mix the icing sugar with enough juice to make it a pourable consistency. Remove the cake from the tin, drizzle over the icing and scatter with the almonds.

Plum and Almond Traybake

Serve at room temperature with a cup of tea, or warm
with ice cream for a comforting dessert.

350g unsalted butter, plus extra to grease
325g light brown soft sugar
2 tbsp apricot jam
9 plums
4 large eggs, beaten
1 tsp almond extract
275g self-raising flour
2 tsp baking powder
75g ground almonds
Icing sugar, to dust

Hands-on time: 30min, plus cooling
Cooking time: about 50min
Cuts into 15 squares

PER SQUARE 395cals, 5g protein, 24g fat (13g
saturates), 40g carbs (26g total sugars), 2g fibre

◆ TO STORE
Keep the cooled cake in an airtight container
for up to 3 days.

1. Heat the oven to 180°C (160°C fan) mark 4.
   Grease and line the base and sides of a 20.5
   x 30.5cm roasting tin with baking parchment.
   In a pan, gently heat 100g butter with 100g
   brown sugar. Once the butter has melted, stir in
   the jam and simmer for 3min, until the caramel
   comes together. Pour into the cake tin and leave
   to cool for 10min.

2. Halve and de-stone the plums. Arrange cut-side
   down in the caramel. Set aside.

3. In a large bowl, whisk the remaining butter and
   sugar until light and fluffy. Gradually add the
   eggs, beating well after each addition. Beat in
   the almond extract. In a separate bowl, combine
   the flour, baking powder and ground almonds.
   Fold into the egg mixture. Spoon the batter over
   the plums and spread to level. Bake for about
   45min or until a skewer inserted into the centre
   comes out clean.

4. Remove from the oven and cool in the tin on
   a wire rack for 15min. Invert on to a board and
   remove the tin and baking parchment. Dust
   with icing sugar, then cut into squares and serve
   warm or leave to cool completely.

Berry Granola Flapjacks

Crunchy, but with the soft chew of a classic flapjack, these are super easy to make and taste just like a berry granola.

200g butter, plus extra to grease
150g demerara sugar
50g golden syrup
300g rolled jumbo oats
100g mixed seeds
100g dried berries, we used cranberries, strawberries
   and goji berries

Hands-on time: 10min, plus cooling
Cooking time: about 20min
Makes 12 bars

PER BAR 365cals, 5g protein, 20g fat (10g saturates), 40g carbs (21g total sugars), 3g fibre

◆ TO STORE
Keep in an airtight container at room temperature for up to a week.

1. Heat the oven to 190°C (170°C fan) mark 5. Grease and line a 20.5cm square tin with baking parchment.

2. Melt the butter in a large pan over low heat. Add the sugar and golden syrup and heat, stirring, until the sugar dissolves.

3. Remove the pan from the heat and stir in the oats, mixed seeds and berries. Press into a tin and bake for 15–20min, until lightly golden. Leave to cool before slicing.

Peanut Butter Caramel Slice

This tasty, nutty treat is surprisingly easy to assemble. Swap the smooth peanut butter for crunchy, for some extra bite.

FOR THE BASE
75g unsalted butter, melted, plus extra to grease
200g Oreo biscuits

FOR THE CARAMEL
25g unsalted butter
200g condensed milk
125g smooth peanut butter
2 tbsp golden syrup

FOR THE TOPPING
75g dark chocolate, roughly chopped
75g milk chocolate, roughly chopped
1 tbsp golden syrup
50g salted peanuts, roughly chopped

**Hands-on time: 25min, plus cooling, setting
  and chilling
Cooking time: about 15min
Makes 16 slices**

**PER SLICE 273cals, 5g protein, 17g fat (8g saturates),
24g carbs (19g total sugars), 1g fibre**

◆ TO STORE
Keep in an airtight container at room temperature
(or in fridge for a firmer result) for up to 1 week.

1. Heat the oven to 180°C (160° fan) mark 4. Grease and line a 20.5cm square tin with baking parchment. For the base, whizz the Oreo biscuits in a food processor until finely crushed (alternatively, bash them in a food bag with a rolling pin). Add the melted butter and whizz/mix to combine. Press firmly into base of the lined tin, levelling with the back of a spoon. Bake for 10min, then set aside to cool.

2. For the caramel, heat the butter, condensed milk, peanut butter and golden syrup in a pan over a low heat, stirring until fully melted and combined. Pour over the biscuit base and spread to level. Leave to set at room temperature for 1hr.

3. Once the caramel has set, melt the chocolates and golden syrup in a heatproof bowl set over a pan of barely simmering water. Once melted, pour over the caramel layer and spread to level. Sprinkle over the nuts and chill to set.

4. Remove from the tin and parchment, transfer to a board and cut into 16 slices to serve.

3

Savoury & Sweet Breads

Malted Seedy Baguettes

Swap the dried yeast for double the quantity of fresh, if you can get it (this will heighten the savoury, doughy flavour). Just whisk the fresh yeast into the tepid water and set aside for 5min before mixing with the remaining wet ingredients.

300g strong white bread flour, plus extra to dust
7g sachet fast-action dried yeast
100g mixed seeds, we used pumpkin, sunflower and sesame
3 tbsp malt extract
2 tbsp runny honey
Oil, to grease

Hands-on time: 25min, plus rising and cooling
Cooking time: about 20min
Makes 2 large baguettes

PER ¼ BAGUETTE 241cals, 8g protein, 7g fat (1g saturates), 36g carbs (7g total sugars), 3g fibre

◆ TO STORE
Once cool, wrap well in clingfilm and store at room temperature for up to 3 days.

1. Mix the flour, yeast, seeds and 1tsp fine salt in a freestanding mixer fitted with a dough hook. In a jug, mix the malt extract, honey and 175ml tepid water. Pour into the flour mixture and knead for 5min, until smooth and elastic. Cover the bowl with a clean tea towel or greased clingfilm and leave to rise in a warm place for 1hr, or until doubled in size.

2. Line a large baking sheet with baking parchment. Once risen, divide the dough in half and flatten each piece into a small rectangle. Fold the corners of each rectangle into the middle, and then roll the dough back and forth into a small, fat sausage (this gives the dough tension, which helps with shaping). Roll each fat sausage into a 35cm length. Lay the baguettes on the lined sheet, pulling up the paper between them into a ridge (this will help keep their shape). Cover with the tea towel or greased clingfilm (oil-side down) and leave to rise in a warm place for 1hr, or until visibly puffed.

3. Heat the oven to 220°C (200°C fan) mark 7. Put a large baking sheet in the oven to preheat for 10min, along with a smaller roasting tin filled with water on the bottom shelf to create steam (which helps form the crisp crust).

4. Carefully remove the preheated baking sheet from the oven and slide the baguettes on to it (still on their parchment). With a sharp knife, cut a few diagonal slashes into the top of each baguette and bake for 20min, until deep golden brown. Allow to cool completely on a wire rack.

Brown Bloomer

Letting the dough rise twice before the prove helps give this loaf a lighter texture.

50g unsalted butter
1 tbsp black treacle
500g strong wholemeal bread flour, plus extra to dust
7g sachet fast-action dried yeast
Oil, to grease

Hands-on time: 25min, plus rising and cooling
Cooking time: about 40min
Makes 1 loaf, cuts into 12 slices

PER SLICE 178cals, 6g protein, 4g fat (2g saturates), 26g carbs (2g total sugars), 5g fibre

◆ TO STORE
Once baked and cooled, store in a plastic food bag and at room temperature for up to 2 days.

◆ TO FREEZE
Once baked and cooled, wrap whole or sliced bloomer in clingfilm. Freeze for up to 3 months. Defrost before eating.

1. Melt the butter in a small pan and set aside until lukewarm, then stir in the treacle. In a large bowl, mix the flour, yeast and 1¼ tsp fine salt. Make a well in the centre, then pour in the butter mixture and 325ml warm water. Mix quickly to incorporate the liquid.

2. With lightly floured hands, bring the dough together in the bowl, then tip on to a lightly floured surface (reserve bowl). Knead until smooth and elastic – about 10min. Form into a ball. Lightly grease the cleaned-out bowl and add the dough. Cover with greased clingfilm (oiled-side down). Leave in a warm place to rise for 45min.

3. Punch down the dough in the bowl to knock the air out, then knead in the bowl for a few minutes. Reshape the dough into a ball, cover and rise for a further 45min.

4. Lightly grease a large baking sheet. Tip the dough on to a floured surface and knead out the air. To shape, flatten the dough into a rough rectangle. Fold the long edges into the centre – this gives the dough strength as it rises. Turn the dough over, smooth side up, and rock it into a bloomer shape (try not to knock out the air). Transfer to the prepared baking sheet and cover loosely with greased clingfilm (oil-side down). Prove in a warm place for 45min, or until doubled in size.

5. Heat the oven to 220°C (200°C fan) mark 7. Make diagonal cuts across the top of the bloomer, then sprinkle with a little flour. Bake for 35–40min until the loaf is golden and sounds hollow when tapped underneath. Cool on a wire rack before serving.

Pitta Breads

A very hot oven is needed to induce these versatile breads to magically puff up.

375g strong white bread flour, plus extra to dust
7g sachet fast-action dried yeast
1 tsp caster sugar
2 tsp olive oil, plus extra to grease if kneading by hand

Hands-on time: 40min, plus rising and cooling
Cooking time: about 40min
Makes 8 pittas

PER PITTA 182cals, 6g protein, 1g fat (trace saturates), 36g carbs (1g total sugars), 2g fibre

◆ TO STORE
Once cool, store in an airtight container at room temperature for up to 3 days. To reheat, pop in the toaster until warm.

◆ GH TIP
Wrapping in a tea towel catches the steam, which softens the bread again. Leave this stage out if you want crisp pittas.

1. In the bowl of a freestanding mixer fitted with a dough hook, or in a large bowl, mix the flour, yeast, sugar and 1 tsp fine salt. Add the oil and 225–250ml tepid water and mix to make a soft, but not sticky, dough, adding a little extra water if the mixture looks dry.

2. If making by hand, empty on to a greased work surface and knead for 5–10min, until smooth and elastic. If using a freestanding mixer, knead for 5min.

3. Cover bowl with clingfilm or a clean tea towel, set aside in a warm place and leave to rise for 1hr, until doubled in volume.

4. Heat the oven to 250°C (230°C fan) mark 9 (or as high as your gas oven will go). Put a baking stone or sturdy baking tray on the middle shelf to heat up for at least 10min.

5. Scrape the dough on to a work surface and knead it a couple of times to knock out the air. Cut into 8 equal portions. Working 1 portion at a time, roll each out to an 11.5 x 18cm oval. If your dough is bouncing back, leave it to relax for a few minutes while you start rolling out another portion.

6. Lightly dust the hot baking stone/tray in oven with flour and add 1 dough oval. Bake for 3–5min, until puffed and golden. Remove the pitta from the oven and wrap in a clean tea towel. Continue rolling and baking remaining pittas (making sure baking stone/tray is hot before baking). Cool pittas completely in the tea towel. Serve.

Bagels

This brunch-time favourite originally came from Eastern Europe.

600g strong white bread flour
2 tsp caster sugar
7g sachet fast-action dried yeast
50g butter, melted and cooled slightly
Oil, to grease
1 tbsp bicarbonate of soda
1 medium egg white, lightly beaten
Sesame or poppy seeds, to sprinkle

Hands-on time: 30min, plus rising and cooling
Cooking time: about 35min
Makes 12 bagels

PER BAGEL 215cals, 7g protein, 4g fat (3g saturates),
37g carbs (1g total sugars), 2g fibre

◆ TO STORE
Once baked and cooled, keep in an airtight
container at room temperature for up to 2 days.

◆ TO FREEZE
Once baked and cooled, freeze in a bag for up to
3 months. To serve, defrost at room temperature.

1. Sift the flour into a large bowl. Mix in the sugar,
   yeast and 1½ tsp fine salt. Add the melted butter
   to a jug with 325ml lukewarm water. In one go,
   add the butter mixture to the flour bowl and mix
   quickly into a rough dough.

2. Tip the dough on to a work surface and knead
   until smooth and elastic – about 10min. Form
   into a ball.

3. Grease the cleaned-out bowl, add the dough
   and cover with greased clingfilm, oil-side down.
   Leave in a warm place to rise until doubled in
   size – about 1hr.

4. Line 2 baking sheets with baking parchment.
   Divide the dough into 12 equal pieces (weigh for
   best results) and shape each into a ball. Working
   one at a time, poke a hole in the centre of a ball
   with your index finger, then insert another finger
   from the opposite side and roll your fingers
   around each other to gently open up the hole
   to about 4cm. Put on the prepared sheet. Repeat
   with the remaining balls, spacing the bagels
   apart. Cover with greased clingfilm (oil-side
   down) and leave in a warm place to prove for
   20min, or until soft and pillowy.

5. Heat the oven to 180°C (160°C fan) mark 4. Fill
   a large pan with water and bring it to the boil.
   When the bagels are proved, add the soda to the
   boiling water. Gently open up the bagel holes
   again, if needed. Carefully drop 3–4 bagels into
   the water and cook for 1min, turning midway
   through. Use a slotted spoon to lift them out on
   to kitchen paper to drain. After a few seconds,
   peel the poached bagels off the paper and return
   to the lined baking sheets, spacing apart. Repeat
   the process with remaining bagels.

6. Brush the poached bagels with egg white and
   sprinkle over sesame/poppy seeds. Bake in the
   oven for 25–30min until deep golden. Cool on
   a wire rack before serving.

Tiger Bread Rolls

A yeasty paste gives these rolls their signature cracked look and savoury chew. Use whole milk in your dough for a richer flavour.

FOR THE DOUGH
200–220ml milk
50g unsalted butter, plus extra to grease
350g strong white bread flour, plus extra to dust
   if kneading by hand
7g sachet fast-action dried yeast

FOR THE TOPPING
25g rice flour
1 tsp caster sugar
½ tbsp sesame oil (see GH TIP)
1 tsp fast-action dried yeast

Hands-on time: 25min, plus cooling and rising
Cooking time: about 25min
Makes 8 rolls

PER ROLL 251cals, 7g protein, 8g fat (4g saturates), 37g carbs (2g total sugars), 2g fibre

◆ TO STORE
Once cool, store in an airtight container at room temperature for up to 3 days.

◆ GH TIP
Sesame oil is traditionally used in the topping of tiger bread and adds flavour, but use vegetable oil if you prefer.

1. For the dough, heat 200ml milk and the butter in a small pan just until the butter melts. Set aside to cool until just warm.

2. Mix the flour, yeast and 1tsp fine salt in a freestanding mixer fitted with a dough hook. Pour in the cooled milk mixture and knead for 5min, until smooth and elastic (adding more milk if dough looks dry). Alternatively, mix in a bowl with a wooden spoon, then knead by hand on a lightly floured surface for 10min. Cover the bowl with a clean tea towel or clingfilm and leave to rise in a warm place for 1hr, or until doubled in size.

3. Line a large baking tray with baking parchment. Divide the risen dough into 8 equal pieces and roll each into a neat ball. Place on the lined tray, spacing apart. Cover with greased clingfilm (oil-side down). Leave to rise in a warm place for 45min, or until noticeably puffed.

4. Heat the oven to 220°C (200°C fan) mark 7. When the rolls have nearly risen, make the topping by whisking all the ingredients with 2tbsp tepid water and a pinch of salt – adding more water if needed to get a brushable consistency. Leave to rest for 5min.

5. Flatten the rolls slightly with the palm of your hand, then brush over the topping. Bake for 20min, or until crackled and golden. Cool completely on a wire rack before serving.

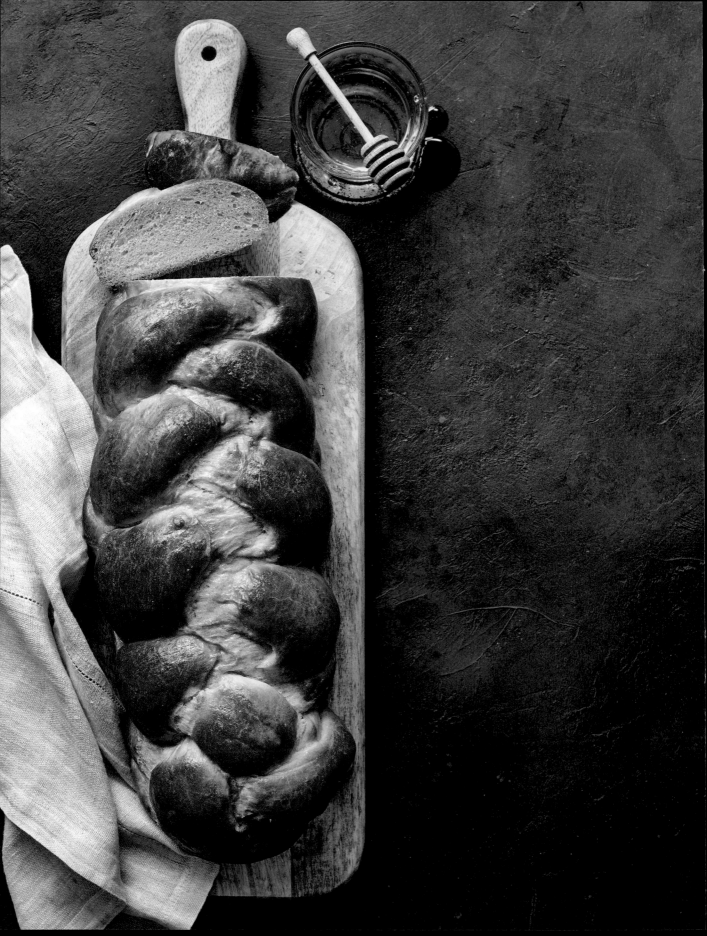

Challah

This bread, usually plaited, is at the heart of many Jewish celebrations, including Shabbat and Purim. The baked golden dough, made here with plain flour, has a cakey texture. Wonderful fresh from the oven or toasted.

FOR THE DOUGH
100g runny honey
10g fast-action dried yeast
150ml vegetable oil, plus extra to grease
2 medium eggs, beaten
750g plain flour, plus extra to dust

FOR THE GLAZE
1 tsp vegetable oil
1 medium egg

**Hands-on time: 30min, plus standing, rising
  and cooling**
Cooking time: about 40min
Cuts into 16 slices

PER SLICE 267cals, 6g protein, 9g fat (1g saturates),
41g carbs (5g total sugars), 2g fibre

◆ TO STORE
Once cool, wrap well in baking parchment or foil and store at room temperature for up to 4 days.

◆ GH TIP
This enriched bread makes for insanely good French toast.

1. For the dough, put the honey into a large mixing bowl (or the bowl of a freestanding mixer fitted with a dough hook) and stir in 275ml tepid water, to dissolve. Stir in the yeast and set aside for 10min, until mixture is foaming.

2. Stir in oil, eggs and 1½ tsp fine salt. Mix in flour to make a slightly sticky dough. If kneading by hand, tip the dough out on to a lightly floured surface and knead until smooth and elastic, about 10min. If using a freestanding mixer, knead for 5–8min. Return to a large greased bowl, if needed. Cover with a clean tea towel or greased clingfilm (oil-side down) and leave to rise in a warm place for 1½hr.

3. Divide the dough into 4 pieces (weigh for best results). Roll each piece into an even sausage, about 45cm long (dust the surface lightly with flour if the dough is sticky). Slightly taper both ends of each length. Arrange the length vertically in front of you, then squeeze together the ends furthest away from you. Always numbering the positions 1–4 from left to right, start by lifting length 4 tightly over the other lengths into position 1. Then lift the length now in position 2 into position 4 (going over length 3).

4. To carry on plaiting: position 1 in between 2 and 3, then place 3 into position 1 (going over the other 2 lengths). Then place 4 between positions 2 and 3 and move 2 to position 4 (going over the other 2 lengths). Repeat this pattern until plaited. Squeeze the ends together and tuck just under the end of the plait. Transfer to a baking sheet lined with baking parchment and cover with the tea towel or greased clingfilm (oil-side down). Leave to rise in a warm place for 45min, until noticeably puffed up.

5. Heat the oven to 180°C (160°C fan) mark 4. To make the glaze, whisk together the oil and egg. Brush all over the loaf. Bake the challah for 30–40min, until deeply golden. Cool completely on a wire rack before slicing.

Goat's Cheese, Rosemary and Red Grape Focaccia

We've suggested using a freestanding mixer for this bread, as this dough is quite sticky, but it can be done by hand. Grease your worktop and hands with oil and knead for 10min, until dough is elastic and soft.

500g strong white bread flour
7g sachet fast-action dried yeast
100ml extra virgin olive oil, plus extra to grease
150g soft goat's cheese
150g seedless red grapes
2 rosemary sprigs, leaves picked
1 tsp flaked sea salt

Hands-on time: 15min, plus rising and cooling
Cooking time: about 25min
Serves 10

PER SERVING 308cals, 9g protein, 12g fat (4g saturates), 40g carbs (3g total sugars), 2g fibre

◆ TO STORE
Once cool, store in an airtight container at room temperature for up to 2 days.

1. Mix the flour, yeast and 1tsp fine salt in a freestanding mixer fitted with a dough hook. Add 75ml oil and 300ml tepid water and knead for 5min, until dough is elastic and soft (it will be fairly sticky). Cover the bowl with clingfilm and leave to rise in a warm place for 1½hr, or until doubled in size.

2. Lightly grease a 20 x 25cm roasting tin with oil. Scrape the dough into the prepared tin and press into the corners with your fingers. Cover with greased clingfilm (oil-side down) and leave to rise in a warm place for 30min, until soft and pillowy.

3. Heat the oven to 220°C (200°C fan) mark 7. With oiled fingers, poke lots of vertical dimples into the dough, pressing down to the bottom of the tin. Crumble over the goat's cheese and scatter over red grapes, rosemary leaves and flaked sea salt. Drizzle over the remaining 25ml oil.

4. Bake for 25min, until golden brown. Carefully remove from tin and cool completely on a wire rack before serving.

Black Olive Ciabatta

In Italian bread baking, the biga is a starter that is left to lightly ferment before being kneaded into the main dough. It helps develop the bread's flavour and airy texture. This ciabatta is best eaten on the day of baking, but you can also freeze it.

FOR THE STARTER (BIGA)
1 tsp fast-action dried yeast
100g strong white bread flour

FOR THE DOUGH
400g strong white bread flour, plus extra to dust
1¼ tsp fast-action dried yeast
1 tbsp extra virgin olive oil
150g black pitted olives, chopped, we used Kalamata

Hands-on time: 30min, plus overnight rising and cooling
Cooking time: about 30min
Makes 3 loaves, each cuts into 8 slices

PER SLICE 89cals, 3g protein, 2g fat (trace saturates), 16g carbs (trace total sugars), 1g fibre

◆ TO FREEZE
Once cool, wrap the loaves separately in clingfilm or freezer-safe bags and freeze for up to 1 month. To serve, reheat from frozen on a baking sheet in an oven heated to 200°C (180°C fan) mark 6 for 10min. Leave to cool a little before serving.

1. The night before you want to bake your ciabatta, make the starter. Mix the yeast and 80ml tepid water in the bowl of a freestanding mixer. Leave for 5min, until frothy. Stir in the flour to make a soft dough. Cover with a clean tea towel or clingfilm and leave to rest in a warm place for at least 4hr, or ideally overnight.

2. To make the dough, add the rest of the flour to the starter with the extra yeast, oil and 300ml tepid water. Mix with the dough hook on a low speed for 5min, to make a soft, wet dough. Add 1 tsp fine salt and the olives, then mix for 5min more, until smooth and elastic.

3. Return the dough to the cleaned-out bowl and cover with a clean tea towel or clingfilm. Leave to rise again for 1hr, or until doubled in size.

4. When your risen dough is ready, wet your hands, then take one side of the dough in the bowl, stretch it up and fold it over on top of itself. Turn the bowl 90° and repeat 7 more times. Re-cover and leave to rest and rise for 45min, then repeat the 8 stretches and folds once more, followed by the 45min rest and rise.

5. Line a large baking sheet with baking parchment. Generously dust the paper with flour to prevent the dough from sticking and being difficult to handle. Gently tip the dough on to the paper. Dust the top of the dough with flour. Divide the dough into 3 rough rectangles using a dough scraper, long palette knife or even the edge of a baking sheet – separating the loaves as best you can. Cover with a clean tea towel and leave to rise again for 30min.

6. Heat the oven to 220°C (200°C fan) gas mark 7. Fill a small baking tray with water and put on the bottom of the oven to create steam. Bake the ciabatta on the baking sheet for 30min, or until golden brown and sounding hollow when base is tapped. Cool completely on a wire rack before serving.

Sourdough

Sourdough bread is made with a fermented 'starter' of natural yeast and is best eaten on the day it's baked. For how to make and maintain a sourdough starter, see goodhousekeeping.co.uk/sourdough-starter.

375g strong white bread flour, plus extra to dust
1½ tsp caster sugar
250g starter (see above)
Oil, to grease

Hands-on time: 40min, plus overnight rising, proving and cooling
Cooking time: 35min
Makes 1 large loaf, cuts into 10 slices

PER SLICE 182cals, 6g protein, 1g fat (no saturates), 37g carbs (1g total sugars), 2g fibre

◆ TO FREEZE
Once baked and cooled, wrap whole or sliced in clingfilm. Freeze for up to 3 months. Defrost thoroughly before eating, or toast from frozen.

1. Into a large bowl (about 25.5cm diameter) put the flour, sugar, 1½ tsp fine salt and sourdough starter. Add enough water (about 150–200ml) to quickly bring the mixture together into a soft, tacky dough.

2. Lightly dust a work surface with flour. Knead the dough for 10–15min until smooth and elastic. Form into a ball.

3. Lightly grease the cleaned-out bowl and add the dough. Cover with lightly greased clingfilm and leave to rise at room temperature for 5–6hr or until doubled in size. Alternatively, after 2hr rising, transfer to the fridge overnight. Remove from the fridge and continue rising at room temperature for 3–4hr, or until doubled in size.

4. Punch down the dough in the bowl. On a lightly floured work surface, knead the dough for 30sec. Shape into a round loaf. Spread out a clean, dry tea towel and cover the centre section (roughly 25.5cm diameter) with a layer of flour about 5mm thick. Put the dough (seam-side up) in the centre of the towel, then draw up the towel and lift the dough into the cleaned-out bowl (allow the towel edges to hang over sides of bowl). Cover the bowl with another clean, dry tea towel. Prove at room temperature for 5–6hr, or until doubled in size.

5. Twenty minutes before baking, heat the oven to 220°C (200°C fan) mark 7. Put a roasting tin of boiling water into the bottom of the oven.

6. Dust a baking sheet with flour. Remove the tea towel covering the bowl, then invert the bowl on to the baking sheet. Carefully lift off the bowl and peel off the towel. Slash a square into the top of the dough with a serrated knife.

7. Bake for 30–35min until the loaf is crusty and sounds hollow when tapped underneath. Cool completely on a wire rack before serving.

Hot Cross Bun Loaf

A twist on the traditional Easter treat.

V

125ml milk
50g butter, plus extra to grease
500g strong white bread flour, plus extra to dust
50g caster sugar
7g sachet fast-action dried yeast
1 tbsp mixed spice
1 medium egg, beaten
250g jumbo raisins and cranberries

FOR THE CROSSES
3 tbsp plain flour

Hands-on time: 25min, plus rising and cooling
Cooking time: about 40min
Makes 1 loaf that cuts into 12 slices, or 12 buns
**   (see GH TIP)**

PER SLICE 294cals, 7g protein, 5g fat (3g saturates),
55g carbs (19g total sugars), 3g fibre

◆ TO STORE
Best eaten on day of baking. If serving toasted,
store in a food bag at room temperature for up
to 2 days.

◆ GH TIP
To bake the loaf as individual buns, shape the risen
dough into 12 balls. Space apart on lined baking
sheets, cover with oiled clingfilm and leave to
rise for 35min. Continue from step 5, baking for
20–25min.

1. In a small pan, heat the milk with 125ml water
   until small bubbles appear around the inside
   edge of pan. Take off the heat, chop the butter
   and stir into mixture. Set aside to cool until
   just warm.

2. Using a freestanding mixer fitted with a dough
   hook (or a large bowl and wooden spoon), briefly
   mix the flour, sugar, yeast, spice and ½ tsp fine
   salt. Stir in the milk mixture and egg to make
   a soft but not sticky dough. Continue kneading
   by machine for 5min (or for 10min by hand on
   a lightly floured work surface) until smooth
   and elastic.

3. If working by hand, return the dough to a large
   bowl. Cover the bowl with greased clingfilm;
   leave to rise in a warm place for 1hr, or until
   doubled in size.

4. Grease a 900g loaf tin. Scrape the dough on to
   a lightly floured work surface and knead in the
   dried fruit. Divide into 8 equal pieces and shape
   into balls. Arrange in the base of the tin and
   cover the tin with greased clingfilm. Leave to
   prove in a warm place for 45min–1hr, until the
   dough is just above the top of the tin.

5. Heat the oven to 200°C (180°C fan) mark 6. Just
   before baking, make the crosses by mixing the
   flour with enough cold water to form a smooth,
   thick but pipeable mixture. Pipe crosses over
   the bun shapes. Bake for 30min, then cover
   with foil to prevent further browning and bake
   for 10min more. To test if the loaf is cooked,
   carefully remove it from the tin and tap the
   bottom – it should sound hollow.

6. When baked, remove the loaf from the tin and
   allow to cool on a wire rack. Slice and serve
   with butter.

Iced buns

These buns are a nostalgic favourite — and the perfect treat with a cup of tea.

125ml milk
250g strong white bread flour, plus extra to dust
250g plain flour
7g sachet fast-action dried yeast
50g caster sugar
50g butter, very soft, plus extra to grease
1 medium egg, beaten

FOR THE ICING
250g icing sugar

Hands-on time: 30min, plus rising, cooling and setting
Cooking time: about 20min
Makes 12 buns

PER BUN 292cals, 6g protein, 5g fat (3g saturates),
56g carbs (26g total sugars), 2g fibre

1. Heat the milk and 75ml water until hot but not boiling. Set aside to cool until lukewarm. Sift the flours into a large bowl and stir in the yeast, sugar and 1tsp fine salt. Make a well in the centre and add the butter, egg and milk mixture. Mix to a soft dough.

2. Tip on to a work surface lightly dusted with flour and knead for 10min until smooth and elastic. Form into a ball. Lightly grease the cleaned-out bowl with butter, add the dough and cover with greased clingfilm. Leave in a warm place to rise until dough has doubled in size – about 1½hr.

3. Line a baking sheet with baking parchment. Punch down the dough in the bowl and divide into 12 equal pieces (weigh for best results). Shape each piece into a 10cm long sausage. Arrange on the lined sheet in 2 rows of 6, spacing about 1.5cm apart.

4. Cover again with greased clingfilm (butter-side down) and leave to prove for 45min or until puffed (the buns should be touching each other).

5. Heat the oven to 200°C (180°C fan) mark 6. Uncover the buns and bake for 12–15min until risen and golden. Transfer to a wire rack to cool.

6. Sift the icing sugar into a bowl and mix in about 1½–2 tbsp water until just spreadable. When cool, tear the buns apart and spread icing on top of the buns. Leave to set before serving.

Chocolate Babka

Rippled with thick, rich dark chocolate, this Eastern European sweet bread is delicious served for brunch.

FOR THE DOUGH
100ml milk
350g strong white bread flour, plus extra to dust
50g caster sugar
7g sachet fast-action dried yeast
1 large egg, lightly beaten
100g butter, softened and chopped into small
   pieces, plus extra to grease

FOR THE FILLING
75g unsalted butter
75g dark chocolate (70% cocoa solids), chopped
150g caster sugar
25g cocoa powder
1 tsp ground cinnamon

FOR THE SYRUP
75g caster sugar

Hands-on time: 55min, plus rising, chilling and cooling
Cooking time: about 1hr 5min
Makes 1 loaf, cuts into 10 slices

PER SLICE 427cals, 7g protein, 18g fat (11g saturates), 58g carbs (33g total sugars), 2g fibre

◆ GH TIP
It's unlikely that you'll have any leftovers, but if you do, you could use them in a chocolate bread and butter pudding.

1. Heat the milk in a small saucepan until just warm. In a large bowl (or in a stand mixer fitted with a dough hook) mix the flour, sugar, yeast and a pinch of salt. Mix in the milk, egg and butter, then bring together into a dough, adding another 1 tbsp milk if it's looking a little dry. Shape into a ball, then knead by hand for about 15min (or about 6min in a stand mixer) until you

have a soft dough that springs back when pressed. Return to the cleaned-out bowl and cover with oiled clingfilm. Leave to prove for 2hr until about doubled in size (or leave at room temperature for 1hr, then transfer to the fridge overnight and complete the recipe the following day).

2. If the dough was kept in the fridge overnight, set it aside at room temperature while you make the filling. Grease a 900g loaf tin with butter and line the base and sides with baking parchment, leaving an overhang to help you get the bread out of the tin later.

3. To make the filling, melt the butter in a small saucepan. Remove from the heat, stir in the chocolate, sugar, cocoa powder and cinnamon. Set aside to cool briefly.

4. Place the dough on a lightly floured surface and roll into a rectangle about 50 x 30.5cm. Spread the filling over the dough, covering it completely. Roll up tightly from one of the longer sides into a sausage shape. Carefully lift dough on to a piece of baking parchment and chill in the fridge for 15min (to make it easier to cut).

5. When chilled, cut the dough in half lengthways so you have 2 long pieces with the inside exposed. Turn each piece so filling faces upwards. Starting from one end, lift one piece across the other, twisting together but keeping the filling exposed, to make one long twisted braid. Push the ends of the twist together to make the length shorter, then squeeze the dough

into the loaf tin (it will seem too big, but it will fit!) Loosely cover with oiled clingfilm and leave to prove in a warm place for 1½–2hr or until doubled in size.

6. Heat the oven to 180°C (160°C fan) mark 4. Bake the loaf for about 50min–1hr until deep golden, loosely covering with foil towards the end of cooking time if it is getting too dark. When the babka is almost cooked, make the syrup. In a small pan, gently heat the sugar and 75ml water and stir until dissolved. Bring to the boil, then remove from the heat. Remove the loaf from the oven, then brush sugar syrup all over the top to soak in. Leave to cool completely in the tin before serving.

Cardamom Buns

These classic Swedish buns are filled with traditional warming flavours.

Ⓥ

300ml whole milk
200g unsalted butter, softened
500g strong white bread flour, plus extra to dust
7g sachet fast-action dried yeast
225g caster sugar
1 tsp ground cinnamon
2 tbsp crushed cardamom seeds, from roughly 25g green
   cardamom pods (see GH TIP)
1 medium egg, beaten
25g pearl sugar (optional)

Hands-on time: 1hr, plus rising and cooling
Cooking time: about 30min
Makes 12 buns

PER BUN 382cals, 7g protein, 16g fat (10g saturates),
54g carbs (22g total sugars), 1g fibre

◆ GET AHEAD
If serving for breakfast, prepare to end of step 6 the night before (but don't prove). Chill overnight. Cover the 2 tbsp cardamom sugar and set aside. To serve, remove buns from fridge and prove somewhere warm for 1.5–2hr, until slightly puffed. Continue from step 7.

◆ GH TIP
You can buy bags of already husked cardamom seeds, instead of doing it yourself. Crush the seeds with a pestle and mortar or spice grinder.

1. In a small pan, heat the milk and 50g of the butter until the butter has melted and the mixture is steaming. Set aside until lukewarm.

2. In a large bowl, mix the flour, yeast, 75g caster sugar, ½ tsp fine salt, ½ tsp of the cinnamon, ½ tbsp crushed cardamom seeds and the cooled milk mixture. Mix well, then turn out on a lightly floured surface and knead for 10min, until springy.

3. Transfer to a clean bowl, cover with clingfilm and leave to rise in a warm place until doubled in size, about 1–1½hr. Meanwhile, in a medium bowl, mix the remaining 150g caster sugar and 1½ tbsp crushed cardamom seeds. Spoon out 2 tbsp into a small bowl to use later. Beat the remaining butter and ½ tsp cinnamon into the larger amount of cardamom sugar. Set aside.

4. Line 2 large baking sheets with baking parchment. Lightly dust a work surface with flour. Punch down the dough in the bowl, then scrape on to a lightly dusted surface. Roll out into a rectangle roughly 35.5 x 45cm, with a long edge closest to you. Spread over the spiced butter mixture, then fold up the bottom so only third of the butter remains visible at the top. Next, fold the top third down over the top of the previous fold.

5. Cut the dough vertically into 12 strips. Working one at a time (keeping the other strips covered with clingfilm), slice each strip in half vertically, leaving the top 1cm uncut. Open up the half-strips to make a long horizontal line, then twist each half 3 or 4 times to make one long twisted line. Holding one end in your hand, wind the strip around your fingers. Slide the loop off your fingers, tucking the end of the strip in to the centre of the loop. Invert the bun on to the lined sheet, ensuring both ends are tucked in. Cover with clingfilm. Repeat with the remaining strips, spacing out the buns on the trays.

6. Cover shaped buns with clingfilm and leave to rise again for 45min–1hr, until slightly puffed.

7. Heat the oven to 190°C (170°C fan) mark 5. Once proved, brush the buns with egg, sprinkle over pearl sugar (if using) and bake for 25min until risen and golden. Meanwhile, in a small pan, heat the reserved 2 tbsp cardamom sugar with 50ml water, stirring to dissolve sugar. Turn up heat and boil for 1min. Set aside.

8. As soon as buns are out of oven, brush with the cardamom syrup. Cool on sheets. Serve just warm or at room temperature.

4

Small Bakes

Raspberry and Rose Éclairs

Replace the rosewater with 1 tsp vanilla
bean paste, if you prefer.

(V)

75g butter, chopped, plus extra to grease
100g plain flour
2 medium eggs, lightly beaten

FOR THE RASPBERRY FILLING
300ml whole milk
3 medium egg yolks
50g caster sugar
25g cornflour
25g butter, cubed
Few drops rosewater
50g raspberries, crushed

FOR THE ICING
50g raspberries
125g icing sugar
Freeze-dried raspberries (optional)
Dried rose petals (optional)

Hands-on time: 40min, plus cooling
Cooking time: about 40min
Makes 10 éclairs

PER ÉCLAIR 244cals, 4g protein, 12g fat (7g
saturates), 29g carbs (19g total sugars), 1g fibre

1. Heat the oven to 200°C (180°C fan) mark 6.
   Grease 2 large baking trays. To make the éclairs,
   melt the butter and 225ml water in a large pan
   over low heat. When the butter has melted, bring
   the mixture quickly to the boil. As soon as it
   is boiling, take the pan off the heat and quickly
   beat in the flour with a wooden spoon – keep
   going until the mixture comes away from the
   sides of the pan into a glossy dough. Empty
   into a large bowl and cool for 10min.

2. Using a handheld electric whisk, gradually beat
   the eggs into the dough to make a paste-like
   mix. Spoon into a piping bag fitted with a 1.25cm
   plain nozzle. Pipe a 12.5cm line on to prepared
   baking tray, doubling back so the éclair is
   2 lines thick. Repeat with the remaining mixture
   to make 10 éclairs, spacing them apart. With
   a damp finger, pat down any peaks.

3. Bake for 25–30min until golden and crisp, then
   carefully remove from the oven. Wearing an
   oven glove and using a serrated knife, slice the
   hot éclairs in half horizontally, leaving one long
   side attached. Return to the oven (opened out)
   for 5min, then cool on a wire rack.

4. While the éclairs are baking, make the filling:
   heat the milk in a pan until just steaming. Beat
   the egg yolks, sugar and cornflour together in a
   heatproof bowl, then gradually mix in the milk.
   Return to the pan and cook, stirring, until thick
   (it will need to boil). Take off the heat and beat
   in the butter. Cover the surface with clingfilm
   and allow to cool completely.

5. Mix a few drops of rosewater into the cooled
   filling, then fold in the crushed raspberries.
   Pipe the mixture into the éclairs.

6. To make the icing, work the raspberries through
   a fine sieve to make a purée. Discard the seeds.
   Mix in icing sugar to make a spreadable icing,
   then spread on top of the éclairs and sprinkle
   over dried raspberries and rose petals, if using.

Speedy Scones

Once you've made these, you might never go back to the
traditional method! Best eaten on the day they're made.

400g self-raising flour, plus extra to dust
175ml double cream
175ml sparkling lemonade

TO SERVE (optional)
Clotted cream
Jam

Hands-on time: 10min, plus cooling
Cooking time: about 15min
Makes 12 scones

PER SCONE (without cream and jam) 197cals,
4g protein, 8g fat (5g saturates), 26g carbs
(1g total sugars), 1g fibre

1. Heat the oven to 220°C (200°C fan) mark 7. Line
   a baking sheet with baking parchment. In a large
   bowl, mix all the ingredients to make a dough.
   Tip on to a lightly floured surface and knead
   briefly to bring together.

2. Pat out the dough to an even 2cm thickness,
   then stamp out 6.5cm plain or fluted rounds,
   re-shaping the trimmings, to create 12 scones.

3. Arrange the scones on the prepared sheet,
   spacing apart. Bake for 12–15min, until golden
   and risen. Cool on a wire rack. Serve with clotted
   cream and jam, if you like.

Beignets

These are delicious little square pastries, served hot with a good dredging of icing sugar. Those served in Café du Monde in New Orleans are probably the most famous in the world, and with good reason: they're pillowy, soft and completely moreish.

7g sachet fast-action dried yeast
75g granulated sugar
2 medium eggs
250ml evaporated milk
50g butter, melted, plus extra to grease
750g strong white bread flour, plus extra to dust
Sunflower oil, to fry
Icing sugar, to dredge

Hands-on time: 30min, plus chilling
Cooking time: about 15min
Makes about 30 beignets

PER BEIGNET 160cals, 4g protein, 6g fat (2g saturates), 22g carbs (4g total sugars), 1g fibre

1. In a freestanding mixer fitted with a dough hook (or a large bowl), mix the yeast, 1 tsp granulated sugar and 100ml warm water. Leave for 10min until foamy.

2. Mix in the remaining sugar, eggs, evaporated milk, melted butter, 1 tsp fine salt and 200ml warm water. Gradually mix in the flour to make a fairly sticky dough. Empty into a large greased bowl, then cover and chill for at least 4hr (or up to 24hr).

3. Fill a large pan or deep-fat fryer one-third full of oil and heat to 180°C, or until a cube of bread sizzles to golden in 40sec.

4. Meanwhile, roll out the dough on a worksurface well dusted with flour to a rough 33cm square, or until 5mm thick. Cut into rough 5cm squares.

5. Working in batches, so as not to overload the pan, fry the dough squares for about 3min or until deep golden, turning midway through. Using a slotted spoon, lift out on to a tray lined with kitchen paper. Repeat to fry the remaining dough.

6. Dredge with icing sugar and serve.

Coffee and Walnut Cupcakes

We've updated this classic combination with a tiramisu-style mascarpone topping to add an extra layer of richness that's bound to be popular!

2 tbsp instant coffee granules
175g unsalted butter, softened
175g caster sugar
3 medium eggs, beaten
175g plain flour
2 tsp baking powder
2 tbsp milk
50g walnuts, toasted, chopped into small pieces

FOR THE ICING
1 tsp instant coffee granules
250g tub mascarpone
2½ tbsp soft brown sugar
25g walnuts, toasted and roughly chopped, to decorate
Cocoa powder, to dust

Hands-on time: 30min, plus cooling
Cooking time: about 25min
Makes 12 cupcakes

PER CUPCAKE 387cals, 5g protein, 28g fat (15g saturates), 29g carbs (18g total sugars), 1g fibre

◆ GET AHEAD
Make to end of step 3 and store in an airtight container in a cool place for up to 1 day. Complete recipe to serve.

1. Heat the oven to 180°C (160°C fan) mark 4 and line a 12-hole muffin tin with muffin cases. Dissolve the coffee in 2 tbsp boiling water and set aside to cool briefly.

2. In a large bowl, beat the butter and sugar with a handheld electric whisk until light and fluffy, about 5min. Gradually add the eggs, beating well after each addition. If the mixture looks as if it's about to curdle, mix in 1 tbsp of the flour. Whisk in the cooled coffee.

3. Sift over the flour and baking powder, then fold in with the milk and walnuts to combine. Divide the mixture between the muffin cases and bake in the oven for about 20–25min, until golden and springy to the touch. Cool in the tin for 5min, then remove to a wire rack to cool completely.

4. For the icing, dissolve the coffee in 2 tsp boiling water and leave to cool slightly. In a small bowl, beat the mascarpone and sugar to soften. Stir in the cooled coffee, then spread the icing over the cooled cupcakes. Sprinkle with the walnuts and dust with cocoa powder.

Honey and Orange Madeleines

Delicate little iced sponges with a real orange kick.
What could be better?

50g unsalted butter, plus extra to grease
100g self-raising flour, plus extra to dust
40g runny honey
Finely grated zest and juice 1 orange
1 large egg
50g caster sugar
75g icing sugar, sifted

Hands-on time: 20min, plus cooling and setting
Cooking time: about 15min
Makes 12 madeleines

PER MADELEINE 117cals, 1g protein, 4g fat (2g
saturates), 20g carbs (14g total sugars), 0.3g fibre

◆ GET AHEAD
Make up to a day ahead and store the glazed
madeleines in an airtight container at room
temperature.

1. Heat the oven to 180°C (160°C fan) mark 4.
   Grease the holes of a 12-hole madeleine tin
   and dust with flour (tap out excess).

2. Melt the butter, honey and orange zest in
   a small pan, then leave until cool but still
   liquid (about 10min). Meanwhile, in a large
   bowl, beat the egg and caster sugar with
   a handheld electric whisk until the mixture is
   pale, thick and doubled in volume (about 4min).
   It should leave a ribbon trail on the surface when
   the beaters are lifted, which should disappear
   after 5sec. For the fluffiest result, start the beater
   on its slowest setting and increase the speed
   gradually as you whisk.

3. Carefully fold in the butter mixture until
   combined, then the flour until no lumps
   remain. Scoop spoonfuls of the mixture into
   the holes of the madeleine tin, but don't
   smooth them out.

4. Bake for 10min until risen and golden. Leave
   to cool in the tin for 5min, then tap the tin on
   a surface to loosen the madeleines. Carefully
   invert the tin on a wire rack and allow the
   madeleines to fall on to the rack. Leave to
   cool completely.

5. In a small bowl, stir together the icing sugar and
   2 tbsp of the orange juice to make a spreadable
   glaze. Use a pastry brush to brush the glaze all
   over the fluted side of the madeleines. Leave to
   set completely, then serve.

Individual Chocolate Ripple Pavlovas

Frangelico is a wonderful hazelnut liqueur, but you can use Amaretto, Cointreau, Kahlúa or even Baileys if you prefer (or replace the booze with 1 tsp vanilla bean paste).

100g dark chocolate (70% cocoa solids), chopped
3 medium egg whites
150g caster sugar
¾ tsp cornflour
¾ tsp white wine vinegar
200ml double cream
2 tbsp icing sugar, sifted
3 tbsp Frangelico or other liqueur
1 tbsp chopped roasted hazelnuts

Hands-on time: 25min, plus cooling
Cooking time: about 40min
Makes 6 pavlovas

PER PAVLOVA 417cals, 4g protein, 24g fat (14g saturates), 44g carbs (43g total sugars), 1g fibre

◆ GET AHEAD
Make meringues up to a day ahead, then cool and store in an airtight container at room temperature. Cover the remaining chocolate and set aside at room temperature. Complete the recipe to serve.

1. Melt the chocolate in a heatproof bowl set over a pan of barely simmering water. Remove the bowl and allow the chocolate to cool completely, but not to set.

2. Heat the oven to 140°C (120°C fan) mark 1. Line 2 baking sheets with baking parchment. Put the egg whites into a large clean bowl and beat with a handheld electric whisk until they hold firm peaks. Gradually add the caster sugar, a spoonful at a time, beating well after each addition. Beat in the cornflour and vinegar, whisking until meringue is thick and glossy.

3. Spoon 6 even dollops of meringue on to the lined sheets, spacing apart. Flatten the tops slightly. Drizzle a scant 1 tsp cooled chocolate on to each and set the remaining chocolate aside. Use a cutlery knife to gently swirl the chocolate into the meringue.

4. Bake for 30min, then turn off the oven and leave the meringues to cool inside for 30min – they should be crisp and peel away easily from the baking parchment. Cool completely on the trays at room temperature.

5. To serve, re-melt the remaining chocolate as before. Whip the cream and icing sugar to firm peaks, then add the Frangelico/liqueur and whisk again briefly to combine. Arrange the meringues on a serving plate and top each with a dollop of cream and a drizzle of chocolate. Scatter over the hazelnuts and serve.

Blackberry Gimlet Cupcakes

Sweet, sharp and juicy blackberries marry beautifully with
gin and a twist of lime in these striking cupcakes.

(V)

175g unsalted butter, softened
175g caster sugar
3 medium eggs, lightly beaten
175g self-raising flour
3 tbsp gin
Finely grated zest 2 limes

FOR THE SYRUP
2 tbsp gin
40g caster sugar
Juice 1 lime

FOR THE BUTTERCREAM
200g blackberries, plus 12 to decorate
2 tbsp Chambord (optional)
125g unsalted butter, softened
400g icing sugar, sifted

Hands-on time: 30min
Cooking time: about 35min
Makes 12 cupcakes

PER CUPCAKE 487cals, 3g protein, 22g fat (13g
saturates), 64g carbs (53g total sugars), 1g fibre

◆ GH TIP
Make a mocktail version by replacing the gin
in the cake mixture with 3 tbsp milk. Replace
the gin in the syrup with 2 tbsp water and leave
out the Chambord in the buttercream.

1. Heat the oven to 180°C (160°C fan) mark 4.
   Line a 12-hole muffin tin with cases (we used
   tulip cases). In a bowl, beat the butter and sugar
   together using a handheld electric whisk until
   light and fluffy. Gradually add the eggs, beating
   well between each addition. Sift over the flour
   and a pinch of salt and fold in, then fold in the
   gin and lime zest.

2. Divide the mixture between the muffin cases
   (an ice-cream scoop is useful for this) and bake
   for 20–25min until risen and a skewer inserted
   in the centre comes out clean.

3. Meanwhile, make the syrup by gently heating
   all the ingredients in a pan, stirring to dissolve
   the sugar, then bring to the boil and simmer for
   1min. When the cakes are cooked, remove from
   the oven and poke holes all over with a skewer
   or cocktail stick. Brush the cakes with gin syrup
   and leave for 5min, then remove cakes from the
   tin and set aside to cool on a wire rack.

4. For the buttercream, put the blackberries
   into a pan with 1 tbsp water. Bring to the boil,
   then reduce to a simmer for 10min, stirring
   occasionally, until the berries are soft and
   their juice thickened. Blend until smooth, then
   pass through a sieve into a bowl. Stir in the
   Chambord, if using, and set aside to cool.

5. In a bowl, beat the butter using a handheld
   electric whisk until soft, then whisk in the icing
   sugar in 2 batches, continuing to beat until light
   and fluffy. Whisk in the cooled blackberry purée.

6. Pipe the buttercream on to the cupcakes and top
   each one with a blackberry.

Churros and Chocolate Sauce

A delicious fried pastry snack that's popular in cafes and street food stalls across Spain. Dip the churros in hot chocolate sauce for the ultimate sweet hit.

75g unsalted butter, chopped
150g plain flour
2 medium eggs, beaten
125g caster sugar
2 tsp ground cinnamon
Vegetable oil, to fry

FOR THE CHOCOLATE SAUCE
100g dark chocolate, chopped
50g milk chocolate, chopped
1 tbsp golden syrup
175ml double cream

Hands-on time: 30min, plus cooling
Cooking time: about 30min
Makes 28 churros

PER CHURRO with 1 tsp chocolate sauce 150cals, 1g protein, 11g fat (5g saturates), 12g carbs (8g total sugars), no fibre

1. Gently melt the butter with 300ml water in a medium pan. Once melted, turn up the heat and bring the mixture to the boil. As soon as it is boiling, take the pan off the heat and add the flour and ½ tsp fine salt in one go. Beat vigorously with a wooden spoon until the mixture comes away from the sides of the pan. Transfer to a large bowl and leave until just warm.

2. Using a handheld electric whisk, gradually beat the eggs into the flour mixture (have patience, it will come together) – the finished batter should be thick, glossy and shiny, and it should drop off a spoon reluctantly when tapped lightly on the side of the bowl. Scrape the mixture into a piping bag fitted with a Wilton 2D or similar star-shaped nozzle.

3. Line a baking tray with scrunched-up kitchen paper. Next, in a shallow bowl, mix together the sugar and cinnamon. Set aside.

4. Fill a large, heavy-based pan around one-third full of oil and heat to 190°C. Carefully squeeze a rough 10cm length of batter into the hot oil, snipping it off at the nozzle with scissors. Repeat a few more times, depending on size of your pan (about 5 churros at a time). Cook (moderating the heat under pan to keep the oil at temperature), turning occasionally, until golden. Remove the churros with a slotted spoon, setting them on the kitchen paper to absorb extra oil, then roll in cinnamon sugar. Repeat the process with the remaining batter.

5. Meanwhile, make the chocolate sauce. Melt all the ingredients in a pan over a medium heat until combined and glossy. Decant into small bowls and serve with the churros.

Nutty Banana Bread Muffins

These make a lovely treat for a breakfast on-the-go, or with an afternoon cup of tea.

FOR THE CRUMBLE TOPPING
25g unsalted butter, chilled
25g plain flour
25g light brown soft sugar
50g pecans, chopped

FOR THE MUFFINS
300g ripe bananas (peeled weight; about 4 medium)
75g unsalted butter, melted
4 tbsp natural yogurt
1 large egg, beaten
1 tsp vanilla extract
175g plain flour
1 tsp bicarbonate of soda
1 tsp baking powder
175g light brown soft sugar
75g pecans, roughly chopped

Hands-on time: 20min, plus cooling
Cooking time: 30min
Makes 12 muffins

PER MUFFIN 298cals, 5g protein, 15g fat (5g saturates), 36g carbs (22g total sugars), 2g fibre

◆ TO STORE
These are best eaten on the day of baking, but will keep in an airtight container at room temperature for up to 1 day.

1. For the crumble topping, rub the butter into the flour using your fingertips until the mixture resembles large breadcrumbs. Stir in the sugar and pecans and set aside.

2. Heat the oven to 180°C (160°C fan) mark 4. Line a 12-hole muffin tin with muffin cases.

3. For the muffins, in a large bowl, mash the bananas, then mix in the butter, yogurt, egg and vanilla. Into a separate bowl, sift the flour, bicarbonate of soda and baking powder. Stir in the sugar and pecans, then mix the dry ingredients into the banana mixture until just combined. Divide among the muffin cases.

4. Scatter over the crumble mixture and bake for 30min until well risen and golden. Cool in the tin for 5min, then transfer to a wire rack to cool completely before serving.

Blackberry and Custard Brioche Buns

Blackberries have a distinctive sharpness that pairs well with both sweet and savoury dishes.

FOR THE BUNS
350g strong white bread flour
25g caster sugar
7g sachet fast-action dried yeast
150ml whole milk
3 medium eggs, beaten
150g unsalted butter, at room temperature, cubed

FOR THE FILLING
300ml whole milk
1 tsp vanilla bean paste
3 medium egg yolks
100g caster sugar
2 tbsp plain flour
2 tbsp cornflour
250g blackberries

FOR THE TOPPING
1 medium egg, beaten
75g pearl sugar or crushed sugar cubes

Hands-on time: 40min, plus overnight chilling, rising and cooling
Cooking time: about 40min
Makes 12 buns

PER BUN 355cals, 8g protein, 15g fat (8g saturates), 46g carbs (20g total sugars), 2g fibre

1. For the buns, put the flour, sugar, yeast and 1 tsp fine salt into the bowl of a freestanding mixer fitted with a dough hook. Mix briefly. Add the milk and eggs and mix for 10min or until the dough is coming away from the sides of the bowl. With the motor on, add the butter one cube at a time until incorporated. Knead on medium-fast speed for 10min, or until the dough is smooth and elastic. Cover the bowl with clingfilm and chill overnight.

2. Line 2 large baking trays with baking parchment. Divide the dough into 12 equal pieces and roll each into a ball. Arrange on the trays, spacing apart, and cover loosely with clingfilm. Leave to rise at room temperature for 1hr, or until slightly puffed.

3. To make the filling, heat the milk and vanilla in a medium pan until steaming. In a heatproof bowl, whisk the yolks with 50g sugar until thick and creamy. Whisk in the flour and cornflour until combined. Gradually whisk in the warmed milk, then pour back into the pan and return it to the heat. Slowly bring the mixture to the boil, whisking constantly. Cook for 2–3min, whisking, until thickened. Pour into a bowl and lay clingfilm on the surface to stop a skin from forming. Cool.

4. Cook the blackberries and remaining sugar in a pan over a medium heat until the berries have softened but are still holding their shape. Set aside.

5. Heat the oven to 180°C (160°C fan) mark 4. When they are risen, brush the buns with egg and roll the sides in pearl sugar or crushed sugar cubes. Bake the buns for 15min, or until turning golden. Remove from the oven and make a fairly deep depression in the top of each bun with the back of a spoon. Fill with custard, then top with the blackberry mixture.

6. Return to the oven for 15min, or until the buns are deep golden brown. Transfer to a wire rack to cool. Eat just warm or at room temperature on the day of baking.

Portuguese Custard Tarts

These delicious tarts with their sweet filling are best enjoyed on the day they are made.

(V)

Butter, softened, to grease
320g sheet all-butter puff pastry
Plain flour, to dust
125g caster sugar
Peeled zest ½ lemon
1 cinnamon stick
25g cornflour
75ml whole milk
75ml double cream
2 large egg yolks

Hands-on time: 25min, plus cooling
Cooking time: about 15min
Makes 12 tarts

PER TART 198cals, 2g protein, 11g fat (7g saturates), 22g carbs (11g total sugars), no fibre

◆ GET AHEAD
Make the custard mixture up to a day ahead. Cover and chill. Complete the recipe to serve.

1. Heat the oven to 270°C (250°C fan) mark 9 (or as high as your gas oven will go) and put a large baking sheet in the top third of the oven to heat up. Generously grease a shallow 12-hole cupcake tin with butter.

2. Unroll the pastry on a lightly floured surface. Starting from a short edge, re-roll it tightly, then cut into 12 even slices. Lightly re-flour the surface and roll out the slices into 6.5cm circles. Line the holes in the tin with the pastry circles, pinching the edges so the tops stick up by 1cm – slightly uneven is fine. Chill until needed.

3. In a small pan, heat the sugar, 125ml water, lemon zest and cinnamon over a low heat until the sugar dissolves. Turn up the heat and bubble for 3–4min until slightly syrupy. Cool.

4. Measure the cornflour into a large jug, then gradually whisk in the milk, followed by the cream and egg yolks, until smooth. Add the cooled syrup (discard the cinnamon stick and lemon zest) and mix well.

5. Divide the filling among the pastry cases, filling to 1cm from the top of the pastry, as the custard will rise as it cooks. Bake in the oven on the preheated baking sheet for 10–12min (or a little longer if your oven doesn't go to 270°C), until the pastry is golden and the top of the custard is browning.

6. Carefully remove the tarts from the tin immediately and leave to cool on a wire rack before eating.

Sugared Ring Doughnuts

If you like, add 1 tsp ground cinnamon to the sugar
you use to coat the doughnuts.

FOR THE DOUGHNUTS
100ml milk
50g unsalted butter
150g strong white bread flour, plus extra to dust
125g plain flour
50g caster sugar
7g sachet fast-action dried yeast
1 medium egg
Vegetable or sunflower oil, to grease and fry

TO SERVE
100g caster sugar

Hands-on time: 35min, plus rising
Cooking time: about 10min
Makes 10 doughnuts

PER DOUGHNUT 303cals, 4g protein, 17g fat (4g
saturates), 33g carbs (13g total sugars), 1g fibre

1. In a small pan, bring the milk almost to the boil.
   Take off the heat, add the butter to melt and set
   aside until just warm.

2. In a large bowl, mix together the flours, sugar,
   yeast, egg and milk mixture to make a rough
   dough. Scrape on to a lightly floured surface and
   knead for 10min. Return to a clean, greased bowl,
   cover with clingfilm and leave to rise in a warm
   place until doubled in size – about 1½hr.

3. Roll out the dough on a lightly floured surface
   until 1cm thick. Cut out 8cm rounds using
   a plain cutter, then cut out a 2cm hole in the
   centre of each. Re-roll the trimmings as needed
   to make 10 rings. Spin the doughnuts around
   your index finger to expand the holes slightly.

4. Arrange the doughnuts on a large baking sheet
   lined with baking parchment, spacing them
   apart. Cover loosely with lightly greased
   clingfilm (oil-side down) and leave to rise in
   a warm place for 20min.

5. Fill a large, deep frying pan one-third full of oil
   and heat to 165°C – a piece of bread dropped
   into the oil should sizzle to golden in about
   15sec. Put the sugar into a shallow bowl. Fry
   the doughnuts in oil in batches for about
   3–4min, or until rich golden on both sides,
   turning midway through cooking. Lift out on
   to kitchen paper to drain briefly before coating
   in sugar. They are best served warm.

4

Classic Cakes

Marbled Victoria Sandwich

For a variation, try adding fresh berries to the cream
layer of this colourful cake.

V

225g unsalted butter, softened, plus extra to grease
225g self-raising flour, plus extra to dust
6 tbsp raspberry jam
225g caster sugar
4 medium eggs, lightly beaten
1 tbsp milk
250ml double cream
75g icing sugar, sifted, plus extra to dust

Hands-on time: 30min, plus cooling
Cooking time: about 25min
Serves 10

PER SERVING 551cals, 5g protein, 34g fat
(21g saturates), 55g carbs (39g sugars), 1g fibre

◆ TO STORE
Keep in a container in the fridge for up to 2 days.

1. Heat the oven to 180°C (160°C fan) mark 4.
Lightly grease 2 x 20.5cm round sandwich tins,
then line the bases with baking parchment.
Dust the sides with flour, tapping out any excess.
In a small bowl, mix the jam with 1 tsp water
to thin it slightly.

2. Put the butter and sugar into a large bowl and
beat with a handheld electric whisk until pale
and fluffy – about 3min. Gradually add the eggs,
beating well after each addition (if the mixture
looks as if it might curdle, add a little flour).

3. Sift over the flour and fold in using a large metal
spoon. Fold in the milk. Dollop over the jam and
gently marble through with a spoon. Divide the
mixture equally between the prepared tins. Level
a little, but don't smooth completely or you'll
lose the marbling.

4. Bake in the centre of the oven for 20–25min or
until the cakes are golden and a skewer inserted
into the centre comes out clean. Cool in the tin
for 5min before removing from the tin and
cooling completely on a wire rack.

5. When the cakes are cool, whip the cream and
icing sugar until the cream holds medium-firm
peaks. Peel off the paper from the cakes and
sandwich together with the cream. Transfer
to a stand or plate and dust with icing sugar.
Serve in slices.

Chocolate Fudge Cake

Our easiest-ever fudge cake is made all in one pan.

225g butter, chopped
225g dark chocolate (70% cocoa solids), roughly chopped
450g caster sugar
175ml milk
4 medium eggs, lightly beaten
150ml soured cream
250g plain flour
1½ tsp baking powder
40g cocoa powder

FOR THE ICING
200g dark chocolate (70% cocoa solids), roughly chopped
50ml double cream
40g golden syrup
200g unsalted butter, very soft
250g icing sugar, sifted
12 chocolate truffles, to decorate (optional)

Hands-on time: 30min, plus cooling
Cooking time: about 1hr 55min
Serves 12

PER SERVING (without truffles) 856cals, 8g protein, 47g fat (29g saturates), 99g carbs (83g total sugars), 3g fibre

◆ TO STORE
Keep in an airtight container at room temperature for up to 4 days.

1. Heat the oven to 160°C (140°C fan) mark 3. Grease a deep, round 20.5cm cake tin, then line with baking parchment. To make the cake, put the butter, chocolate, sugar and milk into a large pan and gently melt, stirring occasionally, until smooth and glossy. Set aside to cool slightly – about 5min.

2. Whisk the eggs and soured cream into the chocolate mixture, then sift over the flour, baking powder and cocoa powder and whisk together. Scrape the mixture into the prepared tin and bake in the centre of the oven for 1hr 45min or until a skewer inserted into the centre of the cake comes out clean. Cool completely in the tin.

3. To make icing, put the chocolate, cream and golden syrup into a medium pan and heat gently until melted and smooth. Set aside to cool.

4. In a large bowl, beat the softened butter and sifted icing sugar using a handheld electric whisk until combined. Add the cooled chocolate mixture and beat to incorporate.

5. Cut the cooled cake in half horizontally. Use some of the icing to sandwich the halves together, then spread the remaining icing over the top and sides of the cake. Transfer to a cake stand or plate and top with a crown of truffles, if you like.

Fruit Cake

This light fruit cake recipe is easy to make as the ingredients are measured with a mug! We used a 250ml capacity mug.

V

1 mug freshly brewed English tea made with 2 tea bags
1 mug sultanas
1 mug raisins
1 mug soft brown sugar
½ mug mixed peel
Butter, to grease
1 mug self-raising flour
1 beaten egg

**Hands-on time: 15min, plus overnight soaking
    and cooling**
Cooking time: 1hr 30min
Serves 10

PER SERVING 247cals, 3g protein, 1g fat (1g saturates), 56g carbs (46g total sugars), 2g fibre

1. Pour the tea, with the bags, into a bowl. Add the sultanas, raisins, soft brown sugar and mixed peel, then leave to soak overnight.

2. Heat the oven to 150°C (130°C fan) mark 2. Grease and line a 900g loaf tin. Remove the tea bags from the mixture and slowly stir in the self-raising flour to make a mixture that's sloppy, but still holds the fruit. Mix in the beaten egg.

3. Bake for 1hr 30min. If it looks as if it's starting to get too dry on top, cover with foil. Allow to cool in the tin for a few minutes before turning out and cooling on a wire rack.

Red Velvet Cake

Food colouring paste – available online and in cake shops – is the best way to give this cake its trademark colour and won't dilute the batter. For a more traditional chocolate cake, leave out the colour.

250g unsalted butter, softened
250g caster sugar
½ tsp red food colouring paste
2 tsp vanilla extract
3 large eggs
284ml buttermilk
2 tsp cider vinegar
275g self-raising flour
1 tsp bicarbonate of soda
40g cocoa powder

FOR THE ICING
275g unsalted butter, very soft
400g full-fat cream cheese at room temperature
475g icing sugar, sifted
Red and white sugar sprinkles (optional)

Hands-on time: 45min, plus cooling
Cooking time: about 1hr
Serves 12

PER SERVING 836cals, 7g protein, 55g fat
(34g saturates), 79g carbs (62g sugars), 2g fibre

◆ TO STORE
Keep loosely covered in the fridge for up to 5 days.
Allow to come to room temperature before serving.

1. Heat the oven to 180°C (160°C fan) mark 4. Lightly grease a deep, round 20.5cm cake tin and line with baking parchment.

2. In a freestanding mixer or using a handheld electric whisk, beat together the butter and sugar until pale and fluffy, about 5min. Beat in the food colouring paste.

3. In a large jug, quickly beat together the vanilla, eggs, buttermilk and cider vinegar. Add to the butter mixture and beat until combined (don't worry if it looks a little curdled). Sift over the flour, bicarbonate of soda and cocoa powder, then fold together using a large metal spoon.

4. Scrape into the prepared tin, level the surface and bake for 55–60min or until a skewer inserted into the centre comes out clean. Cool in the tin for 10min, then remove from the tin and cool completely on a wire rack.

5. For the icing, beat the butter until completely smooth, then beat in the room-temperature cream cheese. Gradually sift over the icing sugar and carefully beat until fluffy.

6. Cut the cooled cake into 3 horizontal layers. Use some of the icing to sandwich the layers together, then spread the remaining icing over the top and sides of cake. Scatter over the sugar sprinkles, if using, and serve in slices.

Best-ever Carrot Cake

The slightly lower baking temperature makes for an even softer and moister cake. When making the icing, make sure the butter is completely soft or you'll end up with a lumpy result.

FOR THE CAKE
225ml sunflower oil, plus extra to grease
225g light muscovado sugar
4 medium eggs
225g self-raising flour
1 tsp bicarbonate of soda
1½ tsp each mixed spice, ground cinnamon and
    ground ginger
150g sultanas
200g carrots, coarsely grated
50–75g walnuts or pecans, roughly chopped

FOR THE ICING
250g unsalted butter, very soft
1 tsp vanilla extract
400g full-fat cream cheese at room temperature
300g icing sugar
Carrot decorations (optional)

Hands-on time: 40min, plus cooling
Cooking time: about 1hr 15min
Cuts into 12 slices

PER SLICE 759cals, 7g protein, 52g fat (23g saturates), 67g carbs (53g sugars), 2g fibre

◆ TO STORE
Keep the cake in an airtight container at room temperature for up to 2 days.
Keep the iced cake in a container in the fridge for up to 5 days.

1. Heat the oven to 170°C (150°C fan) mark 3. Grease and line the base and sides of a round 20.5cm cake tin with baking parchment. Put the oil, sugar and eggs into a large bowl and whisk together until smooth.

2. Add the flour, bicarbonate of soda and spices to the bowl and mix to combine. Stir in the sultanas, carrots and nuts. Scrape the mixture into the prepared tin, level and bake for 65–75min, or until a skewer inserted into the centre comes out clean. Leave to cool for 5min in the tin, then remove from the tin and leave to cool completely on a wire rack.

3. To make the icing, beat the butter and vanilla in a large bowl until completely smooth, then stir in the room-temperature cream cheese to combine. Sift over the icing sugar and mix (carefully at first, as otherwise there will be clouds of icing sugar) until smooth and fluffy.

4. Cut the cooled cake in half horizontally through the middle. Use half the icing to sandwich the halves back together and set the cake on a cake stand/plate. Spread the remaining icing over the top of the cake and arrange the carrot decorations on top, if using. Serve in slices.

Coffee and Walnut Cake

This recipe relies on a strong espresso, so brew
an extra cup of your favourite blend.

250g unsalted butter, softened, plus extra to grease
250g caster sugar
4 medium eggs, lightly beaten
250g plain flour
3 tbsp strong espresso (at room temperature)
1 tsp baking powder
75g walnut halves, roughly chopped

FOR THE ICING
200g unsalted butter, very soft
300g icing sugar, sifted
1 tsp vanilla essence
3 tbsp strong espresso (at room temperature)
About 150g walnut halves

Hands-on time: 30min, plus cooling
Cooking time: about 45min
Cuts into 12 slices

PER SLICE 694cals, 8g protein, 46g fat (21g saturates),
62g carbs (47g sugars), 2g fibre

◆ TO STORE
Keep in an airtight container at room temperature
for up to 3 days.

1. Heat the oven to 180°C (160°C fan) mark 4.
   Lightly grease a round 20.5cm loose-bottom or
   springform tin and line with baking parchment.

2. In a large bowl, beat the butter and sugar using
   a handheld electric whisk until pale and fluffy,
   about 3min. Gradually add the eggs, beating
   well after each addition (if the mixture looks
   as if it's curdling, mix in a few tablespoons of
   the flour). Whisk in the espresso.

3. Sift over flour and baking powder, fold in
   with a large metal spoon, then fold in walnut
   pieces. Spoon mixture into prepared tin, level
   and bake for 45min or until a skewer inserted
   into the centre comes out clean. Cool in tin for
   5min before removing from tin and cooling
   completely on a wire rack.

4. Cut the cooled cake in half horizontally. For the
   icing, put the butter, icing sugar, vanilla and
   coffee into a large bowl. Beat with a handheld
   electric whisk until soft and smooth. Use some
   of the icing to sandwich cake together, then
   spread the remainder over the top and sides
   of the cake. Transfer to a cake stand or plate.

5. Set aside 8 walnut halves, then finely chop the
   rest. Press the chopped walnuts around the sides
   of the cake and arrange the walnut halves on
   top. Serve in slices.

Lemon Drizzle Loaf

Ground almonds help make our gluten-free cake extra soft, but you can replace them with an equal quantity of gluten-free flour to make it free from nuts, too.

175g unsalted butter, softened, plus extra to grease
175g caster sugar
4 medium eggs, lightly beaten
3 lemons
125g gluten-free self-raising flour
50g ground almonds
75g sugar cubes

Hands-on time: 20min, plus cooling
Cooking time: about 50min
Cuts into 8–10 slices

PER SLICE 424cals, 5 protein, 19g fat (13g saturates), 46g carbs (33g total sugars), 1g fibre

◆ TO STORE
Keep the cake in an airtight container for up to 4 days.

1. Heat the oven to 180°C (160°C fan) mark 4. Grease and line a 900g loaf tin with baking parchment. In a large bowl, beat together the butter and sugar with a handheld electric whisk until pale and fluffy, about 5min. Gradually beat in the eggs, followed by the finely grated zest of 2 of the lemons and the juice of ½ a lemon.

2. Fold the flour and ground almonds into the butter mixture, then spoon into the tin and bake for 40–50min or until a skewer inserted in the centre comes out clean. Leave to cool in the tin for 10min, then invert on to a wire rack to cool.

3. Meanwhile, put the sugar cubes into a small bowl with the juice of 1½ lemons and the pared zest of 1 lemon (you will have 1 zested but un-juiced lemon left over). Soak for 5min, then use the back of a spoon to roughly crush the cubes. Spoon over the warm cake and leave to cool completely before serving in slices.

Spiced Pineapple Cake

This modern twist on a retro classic is delicious served with coconut ice cream – soften it first, then swirl through some chopped maraschino or cocktail cherries.

FOR THE SPICED PINEAPPLE
1 vanilla pod, split lengthways
2 star anise
40g unsalted butter
60g light brown soft sugar
½ ripe medium pineapple, about 500g, peeled and cut
    into 3–4mm thick semi-circles

FOR THE SPONGE
125g unsalted butter, softened, plus extra to grease
100g light brown soft sugar
125g self-raising flour
50g ground almonds
1 tsp baking powder
2 large eggs
2 tsp vanilla extract

Hands-on time: 20min, plus cooling and softening
Cooking time: about 55min
Serves 8

PER SERVING 721cals, 8g protein, 46g fat (28g saturates), 64g carbs (51g total sugars), 2g fibre

◆ TO STORE
Keep any cake leftovers in an airtight container at room temperature for up to 2 days.

1. Heat the oven to 180°C (160°C fan) mark 4. Grease a 20.5cm round cake tin and line the base and sides with 1 large sheet of baking parchment, smoothing it out as best you can. For the spiced pineapple, scrape the seeds out of the vanilla pod. Put the pod and seeds into a small frying pan with the star anise, butter and sugar. Cook over medium heat for 5min, stirring, until melted and bubbling. Scrape into the lined tin and allow to cool for 5min.

2. Arrange the pineapple semi-circles on top of the caramel, overlapping them slightly and pressing down in the centre to level.

3. In a large bowl, beat together all the sponge ingredients with a pinch of salt using a handheld electric whisk until light and fluffy. Scrape on top of the pineapple, gently smoothing to level. Bake for 50min, covering with foil after 30min. Cool in the tin for 10min before carefully inverting on to a cake stand or plate. Peel off the baking parchment and serve warm, with a scoop of ice cream, if you like.

Lemon and Poppy Seed Cake

Made with yogurt, this failsafe bake is easy to master
and a true classic.

200g unsalted butter, melted, plus extra to grease
250g self-raising flour
200g caster sugar
1½ tbsp poppy seeds
Finely grated zest 3 lemons
4 medium eggs
150g natural yogurt (not set)

FOR THE ICING
175g icing sugar
Juice 1 lemon

TO DECORATE
Lemon peel (pared or zested)
Poppy seeds

Hands-on time: 25min, plus cooling and setting
Cooking time: about 50min
Cuts into 10 slices

PER SLICE 435cals, 6g protein, 20g fat (11g saturates),
57g carbs (39g sugars), 1g fibre

◆ TO STORE
Keep the cake in an airtight container at room
temperature for up to 3 days.

1. Heat the oven to 180°C (160°C fan) mark 4.
   Grease and line the base and sides of a round
   20.5cm cake tin with baking parchment.

2. For the cake, mix the flour, sugar, poppy seeds
   and lemon zest together in a large bowl. Set
   aside. In a separate bowl, lightly whisk together
   the melted butter, eggs and yogurt. Pour the
   egg mixture into the flour bowl and whisk
   to combine.

3. Scrape the mixture into the tin, level and bake
   for 50min or until golden and a skewer inserted
   into the centre of the cake comes out clean. Cool
   in the tin for 10min, then remove from the tin
   and transfer to a wire rack to cool completely.

4. To make the icing, sift the icing sugar into a
   bowl and add enough of the lemon juice to make
   it a thick and spreadable consistency. Transfer
   the cake to a cake stand or plate. Spread the
   icing over the top of the cake and encourage
   it to dribble down the sides. Decorate with
   lemon zest and a sprinkling of poppy seeds.
   Allow to set before serving in slices.

Triple Ginger Cake

This cake uses a whopping amount of ginger in several different forms, but don't worry – they all meld together perfectly.

FOR THE CAKE
100ml vegetable oil, plus extra to grease
100g fresh root ginger, grated
60g black treacle
100g caster sugar
225g plain flour
1½ tsp ground ginger
1½ tsp ground cinnamon
½ tsp freshly ground black pepper
1 tsp bicarbonate of soda
3 medium eggs
1½ stem ginger balls, finely chopped

TO GLAZE
100g icing sugar, sifted
3 tbsp syrup from the stem ginger jar
½ stem ginger ball, finely chopped

Hands-on time: 30min, plus cooling and setting
Cooking time: about 55min
Serves 8

PER SERVING 361cals, 6g protein, 11g fat
(1g saturates), 59g carbs (36g total sugars), 1g fibre

◆ TO STORE
Keep in an airtight container at room temperature
for up to 5 days.

1. Heat the oven to 180°C (160°C fan) mark 4 and grease and line the base and sides of a 900g loaf tin with baking parchment. For the cake, put the grated ginger into a medium bowl. Whisk in the treacle, caster sugar and oil, until combined.

2. Sift the flour into a separate large bowl and mix in the spices. Measure 100ml just-boiled water into a jug and stir in the bicarbonate of soda. Empty the soda mixture into the treacle bowl and whisk to combine.

3. Pour the liquid mixture into the flour bowl and whisk to combine. Whisk in the eggs, followed by the chopped stem ginger. Scrape into the prepared tin and bake for 50–55min, until risen and a toothpick inserted into the centre comes out clean. Cool in the tin for 5min, then transfer to a wire rack to cool completely.

4. To make the glaze, whisk together the icing sugar and stem ginger syrup until smooth and thick. Spread over the top of the cake and sprinkle over the chopped stem ginger. Leave to set for 5min before serving.

Battenberg Delight

Admittedly it is a little tricky to assemble, but the results are well worth the effort and bound to raise impressed smiles.

175g butter, softened, plus extra to grease
175g caster sugar
3 large eggs, lightly beaten
200g self-raising flour
25g ground almonds
Few drops almond essence
Pink and yellow food colourings
3-4 tbsp lemon curd
500g marzipan
Icing sugar, to dust

Hands-on time: 35min
Cooking time: about 35min
Cuts into 10 slices

PER SLICE 526cals, 8g protein, 24g fat (10g saturates), 68g carbs (52g total sugars), 2g fibre

◆ TO STORE
Wrap in clingfilm and keep in an airtight container at room temperature for up to 2 days.

1. Heat the oven to 180°C (160°C fan) mark 4. Grease a 20.5cm square, straight-sided roasting/ brownie tin. Cut a rectangle of baking parchment that measures exactly 20.5cm wide and 30.5cm long. Fold it in half (short end to short end), then make a 5cm wide fold along the length of the closed side, bending it both ways to mark a pleat. Open up the paper, then pinch the pleat together to form a ridge (so it stands perpendicular to the rest of the paper). Position the paper in the base of the tin – it should line the base exactly and have a 5cm tall divider down the middle.

2. In a large bowl, beat the butter and caster sugar together with a handheld electric whisk until pale and fluffy. Gradually beat in eggs, then fold in the flour, ground almonds and almond essence with a large metal spoon.

3. Spoon half the mixture into a separate bowl. With the food colouring, tint one half yellow and the other pink. Spoon one batter into each side of the lined tin (making sure the paper doesn't shift) and level. Bake for 30–35min or until a skewer inserted into the cakes comes out clean. Leave to cool in tin.

4. Take the cakes out of the tin and peel off the parchment. Use a bread knife to level the top of each cake and remove any browned sponge. Stack the cakes and trim the sides and ends to even them out. With the sponges still stacked, halve the cakes lengthways to make four equal strips of sponge.

5. Spread a thin layer of lemon curd along one long side of a yellow strip, then stick to the long side of a pink strip. Repeat with remaining two strips. Stick the pairs of sponges on top of one other with more curd to give a checkerboard effect. Trim to neaten. Spread ends of the cake with more curd.

6. Roll out one-eighth of the marzipan on a work surface dusted with icing sugar until 5mm thick. Stick to one end of the cake and trim with scissors. Repeat with other end.

7. Roll out the remaining marzipan into a long 5mm thick strip – it needs to be at least 22cm wide and 35.5cm long. Brush with lemon curd. Set the cake on the marzipan at one of the short ends, then trim the width of the marzipan strip to match the cake. Roll the cake, sticking it to the marzipan as you go. Trim the end to neaten. Serve in slices.

6

Savoury Bakes

Caramelised Onion Sausage Rolls

Marmite adds a savoury boost to these pastry rolls, but leave it out if you're not a fan.

1 tbsp olive oil
1 large red onion, finely sliced
½ tbsp soft brown sugar
½ tbsp balsamic vinegar
½ tbsp Marmite
320g sheet all butter puff pastry
225g pork sausages (about 4) – we used Cumberland
1 medium egg, beaten
1 tbsp sesame seeds

Hands-on time: 15min, plus cooling and chilling
Cooking time: about 50min
Makes 12 sausage rolls

PER SAUSAGE ROLL 193cals, 5g protein, 13g fat (7g saturates), 13g carbs (2g total sugars), 1g fibre

◆ TO STORE
Once cool, store in a food bag in the fridge for up to 3 days. To serve warm, arrange the rolls on a baking tray and heat in an oven at 200°C (180°C fan) mark 6 for 5min.

1. Heat the oil in a small pan over a low heat. Cook the onion with a generous pinch of salt, covered but stirring occasionally, until completely soft, about 15min. Add the sugar, vinegar and Marmite and turn up the heat. Cook, uncovered, for 5min, stirring regularly, until dark golden brown and most of the liquid has evaporated. Cool.

2. Line a large baking sheet with baking parchment. Unroll the pastry so a long edge is facing you and slice it in half vertically. Spread half the cooled onion mixture along one long edge of each rectangle.

3. Remove the sausages from their skins and arrange in a line on top of the onions. Brush the pastry borders lightly with beaten egg, then roll up each rectangle from the filling edge. Transfer to the lined sheet, seams down, spaced apart. Chill for 30min.

4. Heat the oven to 200°C (180°C fan) mark 6. Cut each roll into 6 slices, spacing them apart. Brush the pastry with beaten egg, then sprinkle over the sesame seeds.

5. Cook for 25–30min until deep golden. Allow to cool slightly before serving warm or at room temperature.

Goat's Cheese and Fig Muffins

Enjoy fresh from the oven or on a picnic. For extra zestiness, use lemon thyme.

125ml milk
150g natural yogurt
125g butter, melted and cooled slightly
2 medium eggs
250g self-raising flour
50g vegetarian Parmesan-style cheese, finely grated
½ tsp freshly ground black pepper
4 thyme sprigs, leaves picked
150g dried figs, roughly chopped
300g goat's cheese log, cut into 5mm chunks

Hands-on time: 15min, plus cooling
Cooking time: about 30min
Makes 12 muffins

PER MUFFIN 304cals, 11g protein, 18g fat (11g saturates), 24g carbs (8g total sugars), 2g fibre

1. Heat the oven to 190°C (170°C fan) mark 5. Line a 12-hole muffin tin with paper cases or squares of baking parchment.

2. In a large jug, whisk together the milk, yogurt, butter and eggs to combine. In a large bowl, combine the flour, Parmesan-style cheese, pepper, thyme and 1½ tsp fine salt. Stir the wet ingredients into the flour mixture until just combined. Fold through the figs and goat's cheese.

3. Divide the mixture among the muffin cases and cook for 25–30min, until golden brown. Cool in the tin for 10min, then transfer to a wire rack to continue cooling. Serve just warm or at room temperature.

Stilton and Pear Quiche

Tossing the pears in honey helps them stay glossy after baking.

Flour, to dust
375g shortcrust pastry
1 tbsp vegetable oil
1 onion, finely sliced
2 conference pears
2 tbsp honey
3 large eggs
250ml double cream
100g vegetarian Stilton

Hands-on time: 40min, plus chilling
Cooking time: about 1hr 5min
Serves 6

PER SERVING 659cals, 13g protein, 52g fat (26g saturates), 35g carbs (12g total sugars), 3g fibre

1. Heat the oven to 200°C (180°C fan) mark 6. Lightly flour a work surface and roll out the pastry to line a 25.5cm deeply fluted tin. Prick the base well with a fork and chill for 15min.

2. Line the pastry with a large, crumpled square of greaseproof paper and fill with baking beans. Cook for 15min until the sides are set. Carefully remove the beans and paper and cook for a further 10min or until the base feels sandy to the touch. Take out of the oven and set aside. Turn the oven down to 160°C (140°C fan) mark 3.

3. While the pastry is baking, heat the oil in a large frying pan and gently fry the onion until completely soft, about 15min. Peel and quarter the pears and toss in the honey. In a large jug, whisk together the eggs, cream, and plenty of seasoning. Set aside.

4. Arrange the pears on top of the cooked pastry base (still in its tin), then scatter over the cooked onion and Stilton. Pour over the egg mixture. Return to the oven for 40min or until the quiche is set. Serve warm or at room temperature with a green salad, if you like.

Cheesy Spinach Muffins

These unusual savoury muffins will make vegetarian guests feel extra special – and meat eaters will love them too.

100g baby spinach
150g self-raising flour
1 tsp baking powder
25g vegetarian Parmesan-style cheese, grated
50g vegetarian Cheddar, finely cubed
25g butter, melted
100ml milk
2 medium eggs
Small handful fresh parsley, finely chopped

Hands-on time: 15min
Cooking time: about 15min
Makes 6 muffins

PER MUFFIN 207cals, 9g protein, 10g fat (6g saturates), 20g carbs (1g total sugars), 1g fibre

◆ GET AHEAD
Prepare the muffins up to the end of step 2 up to a day ahead. Put the chopped spinach into a bowl, then cover and chill. Cover the flour and cheese mixture and chill. Complete the recipe to serve.

1. Heat the oven to 200°C (180°C fan) mark 6. Line 6 holes in a 12-hole muffin tin with paper cases. Put the spinach into a sieve and pour over boiling water from the kettle until it wilts. Leave the spinach to cool, then squeeze out as much water as you can before finely chopping it. Set aside.

2. In a large bowl, mix together the flour, baking powder, most of the Parmesan-style and Cheddar cheeses and some seasoning.

3. In a separate jug, whisk together the butter, milk, eggs, parsley and chopped spinach. Quickly mix the wet ingredients into the dry – don't worry if there are floury lumps, as these will cook out.

4. Divide the mixture evenly among the paper cases, then sprinkle over the remaining cheeses. Cook for 12–15min until muffins are risen, golden and cooked through. Serve warm.

Asparagus and Almond Tarts

These easy puff pastry tarts make the most
of asparagus when in season.

(V)

320g sheet puff pastry
2 medium eggs
170g tub garlic & herb cream cheese
2 tbsp grated vegetarian Parmesan-style cheese
Zest ½ lemon
24 fine asparagus tips
Small handful pea shoots, to serve
25g almonds, toasted and chopped, to serve

Hands-on time: 15min, plus chilling
Cooking time: about 27min
Makes 6 tarts

PER TART 333cals, 10g protein, 23g fat (15g saturates),
21g carbs (2g total sugars), 2g fibre

1. Cut the puff pastry into 6 squares and transfer
   to a baking tray lined with baking parchment.
   Score 1cm borders on each square and prick the
   insides with a fork.

2. Beat the eggs and brush a little over the pastry
   borders, then chill the pastry for 15min.

3. Heat the oven to 220°C (200°C fan) mark 7.
   Bake the pastry for 12min until puffed. Remove
   from the oven and reduce the oven temperature
   to 200°C (180°C fan) mark 6. Mix together the
   cream cheese, remaining egg, grated cheese,
   lemon zest and ground black pepper until
   smooth. Press down the centres of the pastry
   squares and spoon over the filling, then top
   with the asparagus tips (4 per tart) and bake
   for a further 15min. Scatter over pea shoots
   and chopped toasted almonds to serve.

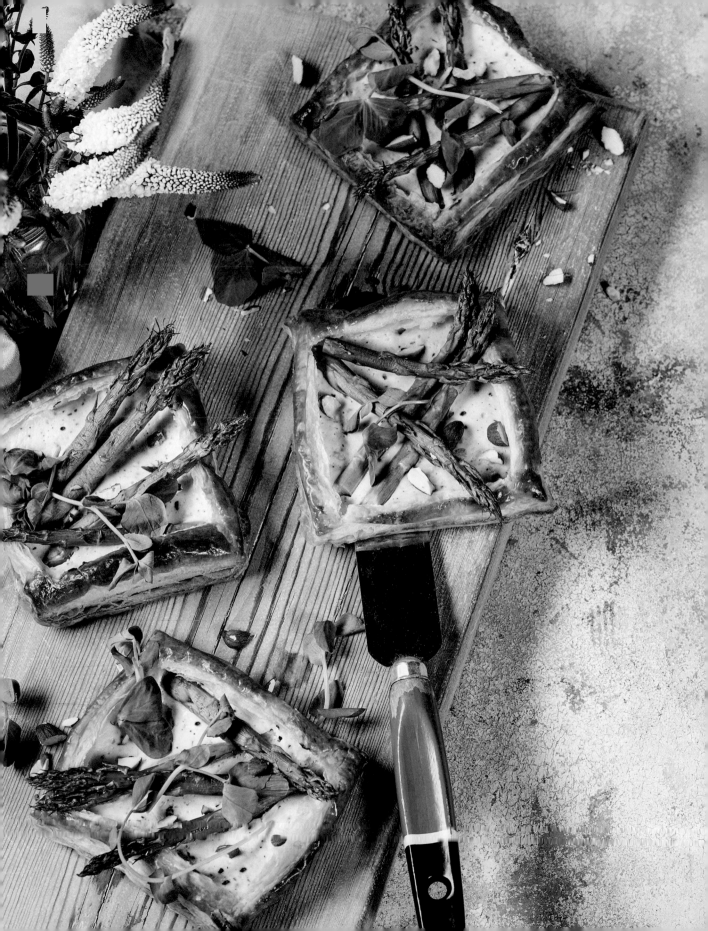

Pepperoni and Pepper Calzones

Have your fillings prepped and ready to go for easy assembly.

700g strong white bread flour, plus extra to dust
2 x 7g sachets fast-action dried yeast
3 tbsp olive oil
75g tomato purée
1 tsp dried oregano, plus extra to sprinkle
1 garlic clove, crushed
Pinch dried chilli flakes (optional)
2 x 125g balls mozzarella cheese, torn into pieces
150g sliced pepperoni
300g roasted peppers from a jar, sliced into thin strips
125g pitted green olives
100g tinned sweetcorn, drained

Hands-on time: 35min, plus rising
Cooking time: about 25min
Serves 8

PER SERVING 554cals, 21g protein, 20g fat (8g saturates), 69g carbs (3g total sugars), 4g fibre

◆ TO FREEZE
Make to the end of step 4. Freeze the calzones on trays until solid, then lift off and wrap in clingfilm. Freeze for up to 2 months. To serve, unwrap and put on baking trays. Cook from frozen at 200°C (180°C fan) mark 6 for 30–35min.

1. Put the flour, yeast and 1 tsp salt into a large bowl. Mix in 450ml warm water and 2 tbsp olive oil to make a soft, but not sticky, dough (add more flour/water as necessary). Tip on to a work surface dusted with flour and knead for 10min. Form into a ball, cover with a clean tea towel and leave to rise for 15min.

2. Heat the oven to 200°C (180°C fan) mark 6. Stir together the tomato purée, oregano, garlic, chilli flakes (if using) and remaining oil.

3. Flour 2 large baking trays. Divide the dough into 4 equal pieces. Keeping the unrolled pieces loosely covered, shape one piece into a ball, then roll out to make a rough 25.5cm circle. Spread a quarter of the tomato mixture over one side of the round, leaving a 2cm border along the edge. Top the tomato mixture with a quarter each of the cheese, pepperoni, peppers, olives and sweetcorn. Season and sprinkle with extra oregano.

4. Fold the plain side of the disc over the filling to cover. Working from top to bottom, roll or fold in the dough edge until it meets the filling. Transfer the calzone to a baking tray and diagonally slash the top of the dough. Repeat with the remaining dough and fillings.

5. Bake for 25min or until golden and the filling is bubbling. Halve each calzone and serve with a green salad.

Beef and Guinness Pie

Slowly simmered beef cheeks become meltingly tender
in this classic pie. Make mini pies or one large one.

900g beef cheeks
4 tbsp plain flour, plus extra to dust
2½ tbsp vegetable oil
500ml beef stock
225g small shallots, peeled
200g chestnut mushrooms, quartered
3 medium carrots, roughly chopped
3 medium parsnips, roughly chopped
Small handful thyme sprigs
400ml Guinness
500g block puff pastry
1 medium egg, beaten

Hands-on time: 35min, plus cooling
Cooking time: about 2hr 30min
Serves 6

PER SERVING 726cals, 48g protein, 34g fat (17g
saturates), 51g carbs (10g total sugars), 6g fibre

◆ GH TIP
To peel shallots more easily, cover them with
boiling water and leave for 1min. Drain, cool
and peel.

1. Dry the beef with kitchen paper, then cut into
   2.5cm pieces (removing any tough gristle or
   sinew). Put into a bowl and toss through the
   flour. Heat some oil in a large heavy-based pan
   or casserole (that has a lid) over medium-high
   heat and brown the beef well – do this in batches
   using 2 tbsp of the oil as needed. Set the beef
   aside in a bowl. Add some stock to the pan,
   then scrape the base with a wooden spoon to
   pick up the sticky bits. Add the mixture to the
   browned beef.

2. Return the pan to low-medium heat and add
   ½ tbsp oil and the shallots, mushrooms, carrots
   and parsnips. Fry for 10min until the vegetables
   begin to soften. Return the beef to the pan (with
   any liquid), then add the thyme, Guinness and
   remaining stock. Bring to the boil, then lower
   the heat, cover and simmer for 1½hr or until
   the beef is tender, removing the lid for the
   final 20min (stirring and scraping the bottom
   of the pan or casserole frequently) to thicken
   the sauce.

3. When the beef is tender, remove the thyme
   stalks and check the seasoning. Divide among
   6 individual pie dishes (each about 450ml),
   or pile into a 2 litre dish. Set aside to cool.

4. Heat the oven to 200°C (180°C fan) mark 6.
   Lightly dust a work surface with flour and
   roll out the pastry to a thickness of 3–5mm.
   Brush the rims of the pie dishes with egg. Cut
   out the lids and crimp on to dishes – re-rolling
   trimmings as needed. Brush with egg. If you
   like, re-roll any further trimmings and use to
   decorate (remember to glaze decorations with
   egg). Cut small steam holes into the centre of
   each pastry lid.

5. Cook for 30–35min until pastry is deep golden.
   Serve.

Build Your Own Pizza

Give your family a selection of toppings and let them create their perfect pizza.

650g strong white bread flour, plus extra to dust
2 x 7g sachets fast-action dried yeast
2 tsp caster sugar
8 tbsp tomato purée
2 tsp dried oregano
125g chestnut mushrooms, finely sliced
50g salami, or other cured meat
83g pack Parma ham
75g sundried tomatoes
3 x 125g balls mozzarella cheese, torn
Basil leaves, to serve

Hands-on time: about 25min, plus resting
Cooking time: about 20min
Makes 4 pizzas

PER PIZZA 1,016cals, 50g protein, 32g fat (16g saturates), 126g carbs (12g total sugars), 10g fibre

1. Put the flour, yeast, sugar and ½ tsp salt into a large bowl. Quickly mix in 350–375ml warm water to make a soft but not sticky dough (add more flour/water as necessary). Tip on to a work surface dusted with flour and knead for 5min. Form into a ball, cover with a clean tea towel and leave to rise for 15min.

2. Heat the oven to 220°C (200°C) mark 7 and put 2 large non-stick baking sheets in to heat up. Mix together the tomato purée and oregano. Divide the dough into 4 balls, then roll each out into a large, thin circle about 28cm in diameter – re-dust the surface with flour as needed. Carefully dust one of the preheated baking sheets with flour, then transfer a pizza base on to it.

3. Spread a quarter of the tomato paste on the pizza base, then decorate with the toppings of your choice: mushrooms, salami, Parma ham or sundried tomatoes and mozzarella. Bake for 10–12min, then tear over fresh basil leaves to serve. Repeat with the additional dough to make up to 4 pizzas.

Great Big Pork Pie

This pie is ideal for buffets and has a surprise layer
of onion marmalade in the middle.

FOR THE PASTRY
Vegetable oil, to grease
900g plain flour, plus extra to dust
250g lard

FOR THE FILLING
½ tbsp vegetable oil
1 onion, finely chopped
1kg pork mince
6 rashers smoked streaky bacon, cut into 1cm pieces
¼ tsp mixed spice
Small handful fresh parsley, finely chopped
4 tbsp onion marmalade
1 medium egg, beaten
100ml chicken stock
1 sheet leaf gelatine

**Hands-on time: 45min, plus cooling and overnight
 chilling**
Cooking time: about 1hr 30min
Cuts into 12 slices

PER SLICE 650cals, 26g protein, 33g fat (13g
saturates), 65g carbs (8g total sugars), 3g fibre

◆ GH TIP
Filling the pie with the stock mixture isn't an
essential step, but there'll be a gap between
the meat and pastry if you don't.

◆ FREEZE AHEAD
Freeze the cooked pie whole or in slices, wrapped
in clingfilm. Defrost in the fridge or at room
temperature and serve.

1. Grease a 20.5cm springform cake tin with oil
   and put on a large baking tray. To make the
   pastry, put the flour and 1 tsp salt into a food
   processor. Next, melt the lard and 300ml water
   in a small pan and bring to the boil. With the
   motor of the processor running, add the hot lard
   mixture and whizz until the pastry nearly comes
   together. Tip on to a work surface, bring together
   with your hands and knead until smooth.

2. Roll out two-thirds of the pastry on a lightly floured
   work surface until about 1cm thick. Use it to line
   the prepared tin, leaving some hanging over the
   sides. Chill for 10min. Cover the remaining
   pastry and set aside at room temperature.

3. Heat the oven to 180°C (160°C fan) mark 4.
   To make the filling, heat the oil in a small frying
   pan and gently cook the onion for 8min until
   softened. Tip into a large bowl and allow to cool
   for a couple of minutes before mixing in the
   mince, bacon, mixed spice, parsley, ½ tsp salt
   and lots of freshly ground black pepper.

4. Tip half the filling into the chilled pastry case,
   then pat down firmly. Spread over the onion
   marmalade, then top with the remaining filling,
   pressing down as before.

5. Roll out the remaining pastry until large enough
   to cover the pie. Lay on top of filling, then trim
   and crimp the edges (ensure the crimped edge
   sits inside the perimeter of the tin or the pie will
   be hard to remove). Brush the top with beaten
   egg (but don't brush outer edge of the crimping
   as it will make the pastry stick to the tin).

6. Bake for 40min, then carefully unclip and remove the outside ring of the tin (leaving the pie on its base on the baking tray). Brush all over with egg and return to the oven for 30–35min to set the sides and cook through. Take out of the oven.

7. Pour the stock into a pan and lay the gelatine leaf on top. Leave to soak (off the heat) for 5 min, then heat gently until the gelatine dissolves. Empty into a jug.

8. Use the tip of a knife or a skewer to poke a small hole in the top of the pie. Using a fine funnel (or a steady hand) pour a little stock into the hole. Keep adding stock (and waiting for it to absorb) until the pie will take no more. Leave the pie to cool for 30min, then chill overnight. Allow to come up to room temperature before serving.

Courgette and Pesto Tart

If making this tart for vegetarians, make sure to use a Parmesan-free pesto.

Flour, to dust
300g ready-made shortcrust pastry
2 medium eggs and 1 egg yolk
150ml double cream
3 tbsp ready-made basil pesto
3 medium courgettes
Basil leaves, to serve (optional)

Hands-on time: 30min, plus chilling and cooling
Cooking time: about 1hr 15min
Serves 4

PER SERVING 637cals, 13g protein, 51g fat (22g saturates), 30g carbs (3g total sugars), 3g fibre

◆ GET AHEAD
To serve the tart at room temperature, make up to a day ahead, cool, then chill. Remove from the fridge an hour before serving.

◆ GH TIP
This tart also can be made in a 20.5cm round fluted tart tin. Follow the instructions above, adding an extra 100ml cream and 1 more medium egg to the custard filling.

1. Heat the oven to 200°C (180°C fan) mark 6. On a lightly floured surface, roll out the pastry to line the base and sides of a 33 x 10cm rectangular loose-bottom tart tin. Leave the pastry overhanging. Prick the base with a fork and chill in the fridge for 20min.

2. Line the pastry case with baking parchment and fill with baking beans. Cook in the oven for 25min until the sides of the pastry are crisp. Remove from the oven, lift out the baking beans and parchment and return to the oven for a further 5min until lightly golden on the base and it feels sandy to the touch. Trim any excess pastry. Reduce the oven temperature to 180°C (160°C fan) mark 4.

3. In a large jug, whisk together the eggs and extra yolk, cream and 1 tbsp pesto. Season.

4. Peel the courgettes into ribbons, stopping when you reach the seedy middle (discard this), then toss in a bowl with the remaining pesto until well coated. Lay about 5 ribbons flat on a board on top of each other. Roll up into a bundle from one of the short ends to make a spiral shape. Repeat with the remaining ribbons.

5. Pour the egg mixture into the base of the tart tin. Gently set the courgette spirals into the mixture, spacing them slightly apart. Bake in oven for about 40min until set. Leave to cool for 10min before serving warm, or serve at room temperature sprinkled with basil, if you like.

Duck and Cherry Pie

Tender meat and sweet cherries are the perfect
match in this pretty lattice pie.

6 duck legs
25g butter
1 large onion, finely chopped
1 carrot, finely chopped
1 celery stick, finely chopped
3 tbsp plain flour
200ml port
600ml chicken stock
1 bay leaf
2 thyme sprigs
400g tin cherries in light syrup, drained and rinsed
1 tbsp balsamic vinegar
1 medium egg, beaten

FOR THE PASTRY
400g plain flour, plus extra to dust
200g unsalted butter, chilled and cubed
1 medium egg
1 tbsp thyme leaves

Hands-on time: 45min, plus chilling and cooling
Cooking time: about 2hr 15min
Serves 6

PER SERVING 763cals, 25g protein, 37g fat (21g
saturates), 70g carbs (16g total sugars), 5g fibre

1. Heat the oven to 180°C (160°C fan) mark 4. Put
   the duck legs on a wire rack set in a roasting tray.
   Roast for 1hr 30min until it comes off the bone.

2. Meanwhile, in a large frying pan, melt the butter
   and gently cook the onion, carrot and celery,
   covered, for about 15min until soft. Remove the
   lid and increase the heat, then add the flour and
   cook for 1min. Stir in the port, stock and herbs,
   bring to the boil, then simmer for 30min to
   reduce. Take off the heat, stir in the cherries
   and vinegar and set aside to cool.

3. When the duck is cooked, leave until cool
   enough to handle, then shred the meat from
   the bone. Discard the skin. Add the meat to the
   sauce, check the seasoning and cool completely.
   Chill for 30min, if you have time.

4. To make the pastry, pulse the flour and butter
   in a food processor until the mixture resembles
   breadcrumbs. Beat the egg with 2 tbsp cold
   water, then add to processor with the thyme
   and pulse until it comes together. Tip on to
   a lightly floured surface, shape into a disc,
   cover in clingfilm and chill for 30min.

5. Heat the oven to 220°C (200°C fan) mark 7.
   Put a baking sheet in the oven to heat up. On
   a lightly floured surface, roll out two-thirds
   of the pastry into a circle about 5mm and use
   to line a 1.6 litre pie dish, leaving the excess
   overhanging. Add filling, then brush the border
   on the pie rim with egg.

6. For the lattice top, roll the remaining pastry
   into a circle large enough to cover the pie dish.
   Cut the circle into strips 2cm wide. Lay them
   over the pie in a lattice pattern, lightly pressing
   down the ends to the pastry case to seal. Trim
   off any excess pastry, then brush the visible
   pastry with beaten egg.

7. Cook on the baking sheet in the oven for 20min,
   then reduce the temperature to 200°C (180°C fan)
   mark 6 and continue to cook for a further 25min,
   until golden and piping hot in the centre. Serve.

7

Special
Occasions

BIG CELEBRATIONS

Chocolate and Fruit Cake

The rich chocolate cake with white chocolate buttercream that opens this chapter is a definite crowd-pleaser. And whether you want to make a single-layer birthday cake or a five-tier wedding extravaganza, it's easy to adapt!

350g butter, chopped, plus extra to grease
350g dark chocolate (70% cocoa solids), chopped
275ml milk
375g plain flour
3 tsp baking powder
60g cocoa powder
750g caster sugar
6 medium eggs
250ml soured cream

TO DECORATE
White Chocolate Buttercream Filling (see recipe, far right)
Chocolate and Fruit Decoration (see recipe, far right)

Hands-on time: 25min, plus cooling
Cooking time: about 2hr
Serves 40

PER SERVING (without filling/decoration) 252cals, 3g protein, 12g fat (7g saturates), 32g carbs (25g total sugars), 1g fibre

PER SERVING (including filling/decoration) 417cals, 4g protein, 21g fat (1g saturates), 52g carbs (45g total sugars), 1g fibre

◆ GET AHEAD
Make up to 3 days ahead. Cool in the tin, then take out and wrap in baking parchment, followed by a layer of aluminium foil. Alternatively, freeze the wrapped cake for up to 2 months. Defrost at cool room temperature, ice and decorate.

1. Heat the oven to 160°C (140°C fan) mark 3. Grease and line a 25.5cm round cake tin with baking parchment. Put the butter, chocolate and milk into a pan and gently melt until smooth and glossy. Set aside to cool slightly.

2. Meanwhile, sift the flour, baking and cocoa powders into a large bowl, then stir in the sugar. In a separate large jug, mix together the eggs and soured cream. Pour both the chocolate and egg mixtures into the flour bowl, whisking well until combined.

3. Pour the cake mixture into the prepared tin and bake in the centre of the oven for about 2hr, or until a skewer inserted into the centre comes out clean. Allow to cool completely in the tin. Finish your cake with White Chocolate Buttercream Filling and our Chocolate and Fruit Decoration (see right).

White Chocolate Buttercream Filling

175g white chocolate, chopped
250g unsalted butter, softened
500g icing sugar
3 tbsp milk

1. Melt the white chocolate in a heatproof bowl set over a pan of gently simmering water. When melted and smooth, take off the heat and set aside to cool for 15min.

2. Put the softened butter into a separate large bowl and sift over the icing sugar. Starting slowly, beat together using a handheld electric whisk until fluffy and combined. Beat in cooled white chocolate and milk.

3. When ready to decorate, use a breadknife to level the top of your cake, if necessary, then slice it in half horizontally.

4. Spread about half the buttercream over the bottom half of the cake, then sandwich it back together. Next, smear a little buttercream on a cake board the same size as your cake (we used a 4mm hardboard) and stick the cake to the board. Spread the remaining buttercream sparingly over the cake and decorate.

Hands-on time: 45min, plus cooling
Makes enough to fill and ice a 25.5cm cake

Chocolate and Fruit Decoration

350g dark chocolate (70% cocoa solids), chopped
White chocolate buttercream (see recipe, left)
Mixed berries (we used raspberries, strawberries, blackberries and blueberries)
Icing sugar, to dust

1. Cover 2 large baking sheets or trays with baking parchment and secure in place with tape.

2. Melt the chocolate in a bowl set over a pan of simmering water. When smooth, take off the heat and pour half on to each sheet. Spread out the chocolate so it's just shorter than the baking sheet in length, and twice the height of your cake plus 7.5cm wide. Chill for 10min.

3. Using a large, non-serrated knife, trim the edges of chocolate to neaten, then cut in half lengthways. Now cut across the rectangles in parallel lines, about 4cm apart. Trim one end of each small rectangle at an angle, if you like, then chill until solid.

4. Buttercream your cake following the method at left. Then, working quickly before the buttercream sets, stick the chocolate shards to the side of the cake.

5. Arrange berries to cover the surface of the cake and dust lightly with icing sugar.

Hands-on time: 45min, plus chilling
Makes enough to decorate a 25.5cm cake

Strawberry Chocolate Celebration Cake

This cake is surprisingly simple to make, but the fragrant buttercream and chocolate glaze transform it into a wow-factor showstopper.

FOR THE CAKE
Unsalted butter, to grease
175g good-quality cocoa powder, sifted, plus
    extra to dust
350g plain flour
500g granulated sugar
1 tsp bicarbonate of soda
2 tsp baking powder
100ml vegetable oil
300ml tub soured cream
350ml hot strong coffee
6 medium eggs, beaten
1 tbsp vanilla extract

FOR THE BUTTERCREAM
200g hulled strawberries
400g unsalted butter, softened
800g icing sugar

FOR THE DRIP
75g dark chocolate, chopped
50g unsalted butter

TO DECORATE
Whole strawberries

Hands-on time: 40min, plus cooling and chilling
Cooking time: about 1hr
Serves 20

PER SERVING 630cals, 7g protein, 30g fat (16g saturates), 83g carbs (68g total sugars), 3g fibre

◆ GET AHEAD
Make the cakes up to a day ahead. Once cool, wrap in clingfilm and store at room temperature. Make the buttercream up to a day ahead. Cover and chill. To assemble, allow the buttercream to come up to room temperature, beating to recombine if needed.

1. Heat the oven to 180°C (160°C fan) mark 4. Grease the sides of 2 x 20.5cm round cake tins with butter, then dust the sides with cocoa powder (tapping out excess). Line the bases with baking parchment.

2. For the cake, mix the flour, sugar, cocoa powder, bicarbonate of soda, baking powder and a large pinch of fine salt in a large bowl. In a separate jug, mix the oil, soured cream, coffee, eggs and vanilla extract. Add the wet ingredients to the dry bowl and whisk to combine.

3. Divide the mixture evenly between the cake tins and bake for 50–55min, until a skewer inserted into the centre of the cakes comes out clean. Cool the cakes in their tins for 5min, then transfer to a wire rack to cool completely.

4. For the buttercream, roughly chop the berries and whizz to a purée. Set aside. Using a freestanding mixer fitted with the paddle attachment (or a handheld electric whisk and a large bowl), beat the butter to soften. Sift in half the icing sugar and slowly beat to combine. Sift in the remaining icing sugar, add strawberry purée and beat slowly to combine. Turn up the speed and beat for 30sec until light and fluffy.

5. Trim the cakes to level, if needed, then slice each cake in half horizontally. Sandwich all 4 layers together using roughly half the buttercream. Next, spread a scant layer of buttercream over the top and sides of cake. Chill for 20min. Transfer to a cake stand or board.

6. Neatly spread over the remaining buttercream. Chill again for 20min. Meanwhile, make the drip. Melt the chocolate and butter in a heatproof bowl set over a pan of barely simmering water, stirring until melted. Cool for 5min.

7. Pour the drip over the chilled iced cake, encouraging it to drip down the sides. Allow to set for 15min before decorating with whole strawberries. Serve in slices.

◆ TO STORE
Cover and store in the fridge for up to 3 days. Allow to come to room temperature before serving.

Jamaican Ginger Cake

We've taken the much-loved spiced loaf and turned it into a dramatic layered cake. And as it tastes better the day after you've baked it, it's a great one to make ahead.

FOR THE CAKE
375g unsalted butter, chopped, plus extra to grease
600g self-raising flour
1½ tbsp ground ginger
1½ tsp ground cinnamon
1 tbsp mixed spice
225g black treacle
225g golden syrup
150g light brown soft sugar
75ml milk
6 medium eggs, beaten

FOR THE BUTTERCREAM
250g unsalted butter, softened
500g icing sugar, sifted
½ tsp mixed spice
2 tbsp milk

FOR THE DRIP
125ml double cream
50g unsalted butter, chopped
100g light brown soft sugar

Hands-on time: 45min, plus cooling and chilling
Cooking time: about 1hr
Serves 20

PER SERVING 625cals, 6g protein, 33g fat (20g saturates), 76g carbs (53g total sugars), 1g fibre

◆ TO STORE
Keep in an airtight container at room temperature for up to 3 days.

◆ GET AHEAD
Prepare to the end of step 3 up to a day ahead. Wrap the cooled cakes (still in their tins) in clingfilm and store at room temperature. Complete the recipe to serve.

1. Heat the oven to 180°C (160°C fan) mark 4. Grease 2 x 20.5cm round, deep cake tins and line with baking parchment. For the cake, mix the flour and the spices together in a large bowl.

2. In a medium pan, heat the butter, treacle, syrup and sugar, whisking occasionally, until melted and combined. Remove from the heat and leave to cool slightly before mixing in the milk and eggs.

3. Make a well in the centre of the flour mixture, then add the butter mixture and whisk to combine into a smooth batter. Divide between the lined tins and bake for 45min, or until a skewer inserted into the centre of the cakes comes out clean. Leave to cool completely in the tins.

4. For the buttercream, beat the butter in a large bowl using a handheld electric whisk until pale and fluffy. Beat in the icing sugar, a third at a time, mixing well after each addition. Beat in the mixed spice and milk until pale and fluffy, then set aside until needed.

5. Slice the cooled cakes in half horizontally. Sandwich them back together with generous layers of buttercream. Scantly cover the top and sides of the cake with the remaining buttercream, smoothing with a palette knife to finish. You should still be able to see the cake through the icing in places (this is what's known as a 'naked cake'). Chill for 30min.

6. For the drip, heat the cream, butter and sugar in a small pan over a low heat until the butter melts. Turn up the heat to medium and bubble for 6min, stirring occasionally, until thickened. Set aside to cool, stirring occasionally, for 10min.

7. Pour the cooled drip over the top of the cake, smoothing with a palette knife and encouraging the drips to fall over the sides. Serve in slices.

Raspberry and Fizz Celebration Cake

This cake is a sensational centrepiece. Use Cava, Prosecco, Champagne or elderflower pressé for the fizz.

FOR THE CAKE
500g unsalted butter, softened, plus extra to grease
500g golden caster sugar
2 tbsp vanilla extract
8 large eggs
500g self-raising flour
1 tsp baking powder
200g raspberries, roughly chopped
4 tbsp fizz, at room temperature

FOR THE FIZZ SYRUP
150ml fizz
50g golden caster sugar

FOR THE BUTTERCREAM AND FILLING
400g unsalted butter, softened
400g icing sugar, sieved
1 tsp vanilla extract
3 tbsp fizz, at room temperature
100g raspberries
Pink food colouring paste

FOR THE DECORATION
150g white chocolate, chopped
75ml double cream
Mixed berries

Hands-on time: 1hr 15min, plus cooling and chilling
Cooking time: about 1hr 40min
Serves 30

PER SERVING 392cals, 4g protein, 19g fat (12g saturates), 48g carbs (35g total sugars), 1g fibre

1. Heat the oven to 170°C (150°C fan) mark 3. Grease and line 2 x 20.5cm round, deep cake tins with baking parchment. For the cakes, beat the butter, sugar and vanilla together in a free-standing mixer, or in a large bowl using a handheld electric whisk, until light and fluffy. Add the eggs one at time, beating well after each addition. Beat in a little of the flour if the mixture looks as if it might curdle.

2. Fold in the remaining flour and baking powder, then the raspberries and fizz. Divide equally between the tins, level and bake for 1½hr or until golden and a skewer inserted into the centre comes out clean. Transfer to a wire rack to cool in the tins.

3. Remove the cakes from the tins and level the tops if needed. Cut the cakes in half horizontally to make 4 layers.

4. To make the syrup, gently heat the fizz and sugar in a small pan to dissolve the sugar. Bring to the boil and simmer for 5min, until thickened. Cool slightly, then pour the syrup over the cut side of each cake.

Continues over the page...

5. To make the buttercream, beat the butter in a free-standing mixer (or in a large bowl using a handheld electric whisk) until light and creamy. Beat in the icing sugar in stages until combined. Add the vanilla and 2 tbsp fizz, beating between each addition, until smooth. In a separate small bowl, mash together the raspberries and remaining 1 tbsp fizz.

6. To assemble, transfer 200g buttercream to a bowl. Use a little to secure first cake layer (cut-side up) to a stand or board. Spread the cut side with a scant layer of this buttercream, then spread over a third of the mashed raspberry mixture. Top with the next cake layer, cut-side down. Repeat, stacking the cakes with a scant buttercream layer and raspberry mix between each and finishing with a cake layer (cut-side down).

7. Spread the remainder of the measured buttercream thinly over the top and sides of the cake to secure crumbs and make the final icing smoother. Chill for 30min.

8. Divide the remaining buttercream into 3 bowls. Use food colouring to dye 2 of the buttercream portions pink – 1 a lighter shade than the other. Transfer all 3 icings to piping bags.

9. Pipe short lines of buttercream in all 3 colours over the sides and top of the cake, then use a palette knife or cake smoother to blur the lines and create a watercolour effect. Fill in any gaps with colour, then smooth with palette knife until you are happy with your effect. Chill for 30min.

10. To decorate, melt the chocolate and cream in a medium bowl set over barely simmering water. Once melted, allow to cool slightly, then pour over the cake. Smooth the top with a clean palette knife and encourage it to drip over the edges. Top with berries to serve.

◆ GET AHEAD
Make the cakes up to 2 days ahead. When cool, wrap well in clingfilm. Assemble up to a day ahead (but don't decorate with berries) and store in a cool place, or in the fridge. Top with berries to serve. Wrapped cakes can be frozen for up to 3 months. Defrost fully, then complete the recipe.

White Chocolate and Hazelnut Cake

A tempting combination of white chocolate and hazelnuts means this elegant cake tastes as wonderful as it looks.

FOR THE CAKE
500g unsalted butter, softened, plus extra to grease
150g chopped roasted hazelnuts
550g caster sugar
1 tsp vanilla bean paste
10 medium eggs
525g plain flour
2½ tsp baking powder
100ml milk

FOR THE CARAMELISED NUTS (optional)
8 blanched hazelnuts
50g caster sugar
¾ tbsp golden syrup
1 large orange
8 wooden skewers/cocktail sticks

FOR THE BUTTERCREAM
100g white chocolate, roughly chopped
6 medium egg whites
250g caster sugar
300g unsalted butter, chopped and softened

FOR THE DRIP
100ml double cream
125g white chocolate, roughly chopped

Hands-on time: 1hr, plus cooling and chilling
Cooking time: about 1hr 15min
Serves 20

PER SERVING 551cals, 9g protein, 27g fat (13g saturates), 68g carbs (48g total sugars), 2g fibre

◆ GET AHEAD
Make the buttercream up to a day ahead, then cover and chill in the fridge. Bring up to room temperature and beat well before decorating.

1. Heat the oven to 180°C (160°C fan) mark 4. For the cake, grease and line two 20.5cm round, deep cake tins with baking parchment. Whizz the hazelnuts and 25g of the sugar in a food processor until fairly fine, then set aside. Beat the butter and remaining 525g sugar in a freestanding mixer (or in a large bowl with a handheld electric whisk) until pale and fluffy.

2. Beat in the vanilla, followed by the eggs, one at a time, adding a little of the flour if the mixture looks as if it's starting to curdle. Fold through the ground hazelnuts, then the flour and baking powder, followed by the milk. Divide the mixture between the lined tins, smooth to level and bake for 50–55min, or until a skewer inserted into the centre comes out clean. Cool in the tins.

3. If making the caramelised nuts, toast them in a dry, small pan over a low-medium heat until lightly golden. Empty on to a board to cool. In the pan, mix the sugar, syrup and 2 tbsp water. Stir over a low heat until the sugar dissolves. Turn up the heat to medium-high and bubble for 5min, swirling the pan occasionally rather than stirring, until the mixture turns a deep caramel colour. Remove from heat.

Continues over the page...

4. Put the orange on a baking sheet lined with baking parchment. Stick a hazelnut on top of each skewer/cocktail stick. Working one at a time, dip a nut into the caramel to coat it (tilting the pan if needed), then poke the other end into the side of the orange (so any excess caramel drips on to the parchment). Repeat with the remaining nuts and leave to cool completely.

5. For the buttercream, melt the white chocolate in a heatproof bowl set over a pan of barely simmering water. Set aside to cool. In a separate large heatproof bowl set over a pan of barely simmering water, beat the egg whites and sugar using a handheld electric whisk until the mixture is warm to the touch and the sugar has dissolved, about 5min. Scrape into the bowl of a freestanding mixer, or continue with the bowl off the heat and the handheld electric whisk. Beat on high for 10min, or until the meringue is thick and the outside of the bowl is completely cool. Gradually add the butter, one piece at a time, beating well after each addition (it might look curdled, but keep beating and it will come together). Once all the butter has been added, beat on medium-high for 4min. Add the cooled white chocolate and beat again until smooth.

6. To assemble, slice the cooled cakes in half horizontally. Sandwich the layers back together with generous layers of buttercream. Scantly cover the top and sides of the cake with some of the remaining buttercream, smoothing with a palette knife to finish. Chill for 30min to firm up. Once firm, use most of the remaining buttercream to generously ice the top and sides as smoothly as possible. Chill for 30min.

7. If you like, drag a palette knife in horizontal rings around the sides of the cake to make stripes, removing a little icing. Transfer the remaining buttercream to a piping bag, fitted with your nozzle of choice. Chill the cake while you make the drip.

8. Heat the cream and chocolate in a small pan over a low heat until the chocolate melts. Set aside to cool, stirring occasionally, for 30min. Pour the cooled drip over top of the chilled cake, smoothing with a palette knife and encouraging the drips to fall over the sides. Pipe buttercream rosettes around the top of the cake and top each one with a caramelised hazelnut, if made. Serve in slices.

◆ TO STORE
Remove the caramelised hazelnuts and store in an airtight container at room temperature. Keep the iced cake loosely covered in the fridge for up to 3 days. Allow to come up to room temperature before serving.

VALENTINE'S DAY

Chocolate and Raspberry Fondants

Be careful not to overbake these oozy puddings –
the chocolate sauce and juicy raspberries should
just spill out.

ⓥ

40g butter, plus extra to grease
50g dark chocolate, chopped
1 tsp cocoa powder, plus extra to decorate
1 tsp flour
2 medium eggs, separated
25g caster sugar
6 raspberries, plus extra to serve
Dried raspberries, to decorate (optional)

Hands-on time: 10min, plus cooling
Cooking time: about 10min
Serves 2

PER SERVING 419cals, 8g protein, 29g fat (16g
saturates), 30g carbs (28g total sugars), 2g fibre

1. Heat the oven to 180°C (160°C fan) mark 4.
   Grease 2 x 175ml pudding moulds well.

2. Melt the butter and chocolate together in a
   heatproof bowl set over a pan of simmering
   water. Cool slightly for 10min. Stir in the cocoa
   powder, flour and egg yolks, being careful not
   to overmix.

3. In a large bowl, whisk the egg whites until
   medium peaks form, then whisk in the sugar.
   Mix a third of the egg whites into the chocolate
   mixture to loosen it, then fold in the remaining
   egg whites.

4. Half fill the pudding moulds with the chocolate
   mixture, then put 3 raspberries into the centre
   of each. Top with the remaining mixture. Bake
   in the oven for 9–10min until just set and risen.
   Invert on to a plate, dust with a little cocoa
   powder and sprinkle over dried raspberries,
   if you like.

Croquembouche Tower

The pastry needs to be beaten together quickly, so have the ingredients measured and your equipment ready before you start. Use toothpicks to secure the strawberries to the tower.

Ⓥ

FOR THE PROFITEROLES
150g plain flour
125g unsalted butter, cubed
4 medium eggs, beaten

FOR THE VANILLA CREAM
800ml double cream
4 tbsp icing sugar, sifted
4 tsp vanilla extract

FOR THE CHOCOLATE-DIPPED STRAWBERRIES
40g dark chocolate, chopped
15g white chocolate, chopped
10 whole strawberries (at room temperature), washed
   and dried

FOR THE CHOCOLATE 'GLUE'
175g dark chocolate, chopped
2 tbsp icing sugar

FOR THE CHOCOLATE SAUCE
100g dark chocolate, chopped
150ml double cream
2 tbsp golden syrup

**Hands-on time: about 1hr 15min, plus cooling
   and chilling
Cooking time: about 1hr
Makes 35–40 profiteroles**

PER SERVING (a filled profiterole with sauce) 213cals,
2g protein, 18g fat (11g saturates), 10g carbs (8g total
sugars), no fibre

◆ GET AHEAD
The baked and cooled (unfilled) profiteroles can
be stored in an airtight container for up to 2 days.

1. Heat the oven to 200°C (180°C fan) mark 6.
   Line 3 large baking sheets with baking
   parchment. Sift the flour into a large bowl
   and have a wooden spoon at the ready.

2. Put a pan over a high heat. Pour in 300ml
   just-boiled water from a kettle and add the
   butter. Cover with a lid and bring to the boil.
   As soon as the mix is boiling vigorously, take
   off the heat. Remove the lid and quickly add the
   flour in one go. Beat vigorously with the wooden
   spoon until glossy and the mixture comes away
   cleanly from the sides of the pan in one smooth
   ball. Spoon into the empty flour bowl and set
   aside to cool completely.

3. Gradually beat the eggs into the cooled flour
   mixture until smooth and glossy. Spoon into a
   large piping bag fitted with a 1cm plain nozzle.
   Pipe mounds 4cm wide and 3cm high on to the
   prepared baking sheets, spacing about 3cm
   apart. Use a damp finger to flatten any peaks.
   Bake for 20–25min until puffed and golden.

4. Remove from the oven and, once cool enough
   to handle, pierce the base of each bun with a
   skewer to allow steam to escape. Return to the
   oven, hole sides up, for 3min. Cool completely
   on a wire rack.

Continues over the page...

5. In a large bowl, whip the cream, icing sugar and vanilla to soft peaks. Spoon half the mixture into a piping bag with a 1cm plain nozzle. Pipe the cream into the buns (make skewer holes a little bigger first, if needed) until they are full but not bursting. Re-fill the piping bag as needed. Store the filled buns, covered, in the fridge until needed.

6. For the chocolate-dipped strawberries, melt both chocolates in separate bowls set over pans of barely simmering water. Dip the bottom half of the strawberries into dark chocolate and put on a wire rack set over a baking sheet to collect drips. Drizzle over a little melted white chocolate and leave to set at room temperature.

7. When you are ready to create the tower, put a large, flat cake stand into the fridge to chill while you make the chocolate 'glue'. Melt the chocolate in a bowl set over a pan of barely simmering water, then sift in the icing sugar and stir until smooth. Turn off the heat under the pan, but keep the bowl set over the water while you assemble the tower.

8. To assemble, remove the cake stand from the fridge. Using about 11 profiteroles, dip the bases into the chocolate 'glue' and position on the cake stand to make a circle (make sure the profiteroles sit snugly together). Dip the remaining profiteroles in chocolate one by one, then set them on top of this base layer, arranging them in a conical tower. (If it's a warm day, you may need to chill the tower intermittently for 5min at a time as you work, re-melting the chocolate 'glue' as needed.)

9. For the chocolate sauce, heat the chocolate, cream and golden syrup in a bowl set over a pan of barely simmering water until nearly melted. Remove from the heat and stir until smooth. Pour into a serving jug and set aside to cool for 10min before drizzling over the profiterole tower and serving with the dipped strawberries.

Red Velvet Cupcakes

Food colouring paste gives these American classics their vibrant shade.

150g self-raising flour
1½ tbsp cocoa powder
150ml buttermilk
¼ tsp red food colouring paste
100g unsalted butter, softened
150g granulated sugar
2 medium eggs
1 tsp vanilla extract
¾ tsp white wine vinegar
¾ tsp bicarbonate of soda

FOR THE ICING
125g unsalted butter, softened
300g tub full-fat cream cheese
75g icing sugar
1 tsp vanilla extract
Red sugar sprinkles (optional)

Hands-on time: 35min, plus cooling
Cooking time: about 25min
Makes 12 cupcakes

PER CUPCAKE 341cals, 4g protein, 23g fat (14g saturates), 30g carbs (20g total sugars), 1g fibre

◆ GET AHEAD
Make to end of step 3 up to a day ahead. Once cool, keep the un-iced cakes in an airtight container. Ice the cakes up to 10hr ahead, adding sprinkles at the last minute, if using.

1. Heat the oven to 180°C (160°C fan) mark 4 and line a 12-hole muffin tin with paper cases. In a large bowl, sift together the flour, cocoa powder and a pinch of salt, then set aside. In a small jug, mix together the buttermilk and food colouring paste and set aside.

2. In a separate large bowl, use a handheld electric whisk to beat together the softened butter and sugar until pale and fluffy – about 1min. Add the eggs and vanilla and beat again. Beat in half the flour mixture, then half the buttermilk mixture, alternating until all the flour and buttermilk have been incorporated.

3. In a small cup, quickly mix together the vinegar and bicarbonate of soda, then fold through the cake mixture. Divide among the cases and bake for 25min or until a skewer inserted into the centre of the cakes comes out clean. Transfer to a wire rack and cool completely.

4. For the icing, beat the butter in a large bowl until smooth, then add the cream cheese and sift over the icing sugar. Mix until combined. Quickly beat in the vanilla. Pipe or smooth the icing over the cooled cupcakes and scatter with sprinkles, if using.

EASTER

Iced Easter Biscuits

Condensed milk gives these biscuits extra crunch and helps them hold their shape.

75g unsalted butter, softened, plus extra to grease
100g caster sugar
40g condensed milk
1 medium egg
Finely grated zest ½ orange or ½ lemon
½ tsp baking powder
200g plain flour, plus extra to dust

TO DECORATE
Icing sugar
Food colouring pastes

**Hands-on time: 25min, plus chilling, cooling
  and setting**
Cooking time: about 12min
Makes about 25 biscuits

PER BISCUIT 95cals, 1g protein 3g fat (2g saturates),
16g carbs (10g total sugars), trace fibre

◆ TO STORE
Keep un-iced biscuits in an airtight container for up to 5 days. Iced biscuits may soften after a few days.

1. Put the butter, sugar and condensed milk into a large bowl. Mix with a wooden spoon until pale and fluffy. Beat in the egg and zest, followed by baking powder, flour and a pinch of salt. Bring together with your hands. Wrap the dough in clingfilm and chill for 30min.

2. Lightly grease 2 large baking sheets with butter. Lightly flour a work surface and roll out the dough until 5mm thick. Stamp out Easter shapes, re-rolling trimmings as needed.

3. Arrange the biscuits on prepared sheets. If you later want to thread a ribbon through the top, make a 5mm hole in each biscuit with a skewer. Chill for 15min.

4. Heat the oven to 180°C (160°C fan) mark 4. Bake the biscuits for 10–12min until lightly golden. Loosen with a palette knife, then transfer to a wire rack to cool completely.

5. For the icing, sift the icing sugar into a bowl and add just enough water to make a thick, spreadable icing. Divide the icing and colour as needed. Pipe or spread over biscuits and leave to set. If you like, thread ribbons through the biscuits and hang on branches.

Easter Rainbow Cake

This stunning creation is made with Simnel-inspired flavours. It tastes as good as it sounds!

FOR THE CAKE
Oil, to grease
200g raisins
550g unsalted butter, softened
750g light brown soft sugar
1 tbsp vanilla extract
1 tbsp mixed spice
Finely grated zest 1 orange, plus 1 tbsp juice
Finely grated zest 1 lemon, plus 1 tbsp juice
12 medium eggs
850g plain flour, sifted
2 tbsp baking powder

FOR THE BUTTERCREAM
825g unsalted butter, softened
1.5kg icing sugar, sifted, plus extra to dust
1 tbsp almond extract
3–5 tbsp milk
Yellow, green, blue, purple and pink food colouring
    paste/gels
Mini chocolate eggs

Hands-on time: 1hr 30min, plus cooling and chilling
Cooking time: about 1hr 30min
Serves about 30

PER SERVING (without mini chocolate eggs)
788cals, 6g protein, 40g fat (25g saturates),
101g carbs (79g total sugars), 1g fibre

◆ GET AHEAD
Prepare to end of step 3 up to a day ahead. Once cool, remove the cakes from the tins, wrap well in clingfilm and store at room temperature. Complete recipe to serve.

1. Heat the oven to 180°C (160°C fan) mark 4. Lightly grease 2 x 20.5cm round, loose-bottom cake tins, each about 9cm deep. Line the bases and sides with baking parchment, making sure the paper is 4cm taller than the sides of the tins. Wrap the outside of the tins with a strip of newspaper, 7 layers thick. Secure in place with string and trim to same height as the paper.

2. To make the cakes, bring the raisins and 175ml water to the boil in a small pan. Set aside. In a very large mixing bowl, beat the butter, brown sugar, vanilla, mixed spice and citrus zests using a handheld electric whisk until light and fluffy, about 5min. Beat in the eggs one at a time, beating in a little of the flour if the mixture seems as if it's beginning to curdle.

3. Whizz the raisin mixture to a smooth purée in a food processor. Fold the flour, baking powder, raisin mixture and citrus juices into the butter mixture. Divide between the prepared tins and smooth the tops. Bake for 1hr 25min–1hr 30min or until the cakes are risen, springy to the touch and a skewer inserted into the centre comes out clean. Cool completely in the tins, covered with a clean tea towel.

Continues over the page...

4. In a very large mixing bowl, beat the butter with a handheld electric whisk until soft. (If you do not have a large enough bowl, make the buttercream in 2 batches.) Add half the icing sugar and, starting slowly, beat to combine. Add the remaining icing sugar and the almond extract and beat (slowly at first) until light and fluffy – about 3min. Beat in enough milk to make a thick but easily spreadable consistency.

5. Spoon 1.1kg buttercream into a separate bowl and set aside. Split the remaining icing evenly among 5 bowls (weigh for best results, each should be about 250g). Dye each of these 5 icings to the desired shade using food paste/gels, then spoon into 5 separate disposable piping bags.

6. Remove the cakes from the tins, peel off the baking paper and slice both in half horizontally with a serrated knife. Spread a little of the reserved plain buttercream on to a cake stand or plate. Using more plain icing, sandwich the sliced cakes back together, making sure the top layer is a cake base, cut-side down. (This will ensure the top of cake is smooth and flat.) Use the remaining plain buttercream to spread a generous layer on top of cake and a scant layer on the sides. Chill for 20min.

7. Snip 1cm off the end of each piping bag. Pipe a vertical line of 7 dots on to the side of the cake, each about 2cm wide and 2cm deep, starting from the top and repeating the colours in the order: yellow, green, blue, purple, pink. Using a separate teaspoon for each colour, smear half of each icing dot on to cake in a horizontal line about 5cm long. On top of the smeared icing, pipe another row of vertical dots, starting at the top again with the next colour in the repeated series (eg green). Smear as before, then repeat the process starting with the third colour (blue), etc. (The pattern will become apparent!) Repeat the piping and smearing process until the cake is covered. There will be a tiny gap where the final row of dots meets your first line of icing – make this the back of the cake.

8. Pile mini chocolate eggs on top of the cake and serve in slices.

◆ TO STORE
The finished cake will keep in an airtight container (or loosely wrapped in foil) at room temperature for up to 2 days.

Chocolate Mousse Cake

This light cake is like a set mousse — you can even hear
the bubbles pop as you slice it!

150g unsalted butter, chopped, plus extra to grease
300g milk chocolate (37% cocoa solids), chopped
    (see GH TIP)
6 large eggs, at room temperature
Cocoa powder, to dust (optional)
Double cream, to serve (optional)

Hands-on time: 20min, plus cooling
Cooking time: about 1hr 25min
Serves 8

PER SERVING 396cals, 9g protein, 31g fat (18g
saturates), 20g carbs (20g total sugars), 1g fibre

◆ GET AHEAD
Make up to a day ahead. Once cool, cover tin and
keep at room temperature.

◆ GH TIP
Green & Black's Milk Chocolate has just the right
percentage of cocoa solids and is gluten free.

1. Heat the oven to 160°C (140°C fan) mark 3.
   Lightly grease and line a deep 20.5cm round,
   loose-bottomed cake tin with baking parchment.
   Wrap the outside of the cake tin in 3 layers
   of extra-wide foil, to make the tin watertight.

2. Melt the chocolate and butter together in
   a medium pan set over a low heat, stirring
   occasionally. Once combined, set aside to
   cool for 10min.

3. Using a freestanding mixer or handheld electric
   whisk and a large bowl, beat the eggs until
   foamy and thick, about 10min. Using a metal
   spoon, carefully fold in the cooled chocolate
   mixture until just combined, trying to keep
   in as much air as you can.

4. Gently pour into the prepared tin and give
   it a little shake to level the surface. Place in
   a deep roasting tin, then pour in boiling water
   to come halfway up the outside of the wrapped
   tin. Bake for 1¼hr or until the cake is set with
   only a slight wobble.

5. Allow to cool for 30min in the roasting tin, then
   remove from the water and cool completely.
   When ready to serve, unmould the cake from
   the tin and transfer to a cake stand or plate.
   Dust with cocoa powder and serve with lightly
   whipped cream, if you like.

Marmalade and Chocolate Hot Cross Buns

Sticky-sweet buns with a hidden gooey centre! You can, of course, leave out the ganache balls if you fancy a chocolate-free version.

FOR THE FILLING
75ml double cream
50g dark chocolate, finely chopped
50g milk chocolate, finely chopped

FOR THE BUNS
75g unsalted butter, chopped
500g strong white bread flour, plus extra to dust
7g sachet fast-action dried yeast
1½ tbsp mixed spice
2 tsp ground cinnamon
Finely grated zest 2 oranges
1 tbsp thick-cut marmalade
275ml milk
250g sultanas

FOR THE TOPPING
50g strong white bread flour
3 tbsp thick-cut marmalade

Hands-on time: 40min, plus chilling, rising and cooling
Cooking time: about 35min
Makes 12 buns

PER BUN 373cals, 8g protein, 12g fat (7g saturates), 58g carbs (23g total sugars), 2g fibre

◆ TO STORE
These buns are best eaten on the day they're made, or can be stored in an airtight container at room temperature and served toasted the next day.

1. For the chocolate filling, heat the cream in a small pan until steaming. Put the chocolate into a heatproof bowl and pour over the cream. Leave for 1min to melt the chocolate before stirring. Chill for 30min to firm up.

2. Meanwhile, in a large bowl, rub the butter into the flour with your fingertips until the mixture resembles fine breadcrumbs. Mix in the yeast, spices, orange zest and 1 tsp fine salt. In a jug, whisk the marmalade into the milk, then stir into the dry ingredients with a wooden spoon, until dough starts to come together. Tip on to a lightly floured work surface and knead for 10min, until the dough feels smooth and not sticky. Return the dough to the bowl, cover with clingfilm and leave to rise in a warm place for 1hr, until well risen and doubled in volume.

3. Roll the chocolate filling into 12 equal balls. Arrange on a plate and chill until needed.

4. Line a baking tray with baking parchment. Scrape the dough on to a lightly floured surface and knead in the sultanas as best you can. Divide into 12 equal pieces. Working one piece at a time, flatten out the dough and place a chocolate ball in the centre of it. Pull up the dough to fully encase the chocolate. Put on to lined tray, seam down. Repeat with the remaining dough and chocolate, arranging the buns so they are almost touching.

5. Cover with a clean tea towel and leave to rise again for 45min, or until noticeably puffed.

6. Heat the oven to 200°C (180°C fan) mark 6. For the topping, mix the flour with 4 tbsp water to form a thick but pipeable mixture. Scrape into a piping bag fitted with a 5mm nozzle and pipe crosses on to the risen buns. Bake for 25min, or until deep golden brown. In a small pan, heat the 3 tbsp marmalade with 1 tbsp water until bubbling. Strain into a small bowl, working the mixture well (discard any shred).

7. Transfer the baked buns to a wire rack and leave to cool for 5min before brushing over the marmalade glaze. Serve warm or at room temperature.

Chocolate Bundt

Bundt tins vary hugely in shape and size – just make sure yours holds the same volume as our specification so the cake mixture will fit.

V

225g unsalted butter, chopped, plus extra to grease
75g good-quality cocoa powder, plus extra to dust
250ml strong coffee
300g plain flour
½ tsp baking powder
½ tsp bicarbonate of soda
400g caster sugar
4 medium eggs
125g natural yogurt
1 tbsp vanilla extract

TO GLAZE
100ml double cream
75g dark chocolate, finely chopped
25ml golden syrup
Chocolate coffee truffles, to decorate (optional)

Hands-on time: 30min, plus cooling
Cooking time: about 1hr
Serves 12

PER SERVING (without truffles) 496cals, 7g protein, 25g fat (15g saturates), 60g carbs (40g total sugars), 2g fibre

◆ TO STORE
Keep in an airtight container at room temperature for up to 4 days. (The truffles are best kept chilled, as they will soften on standing.)

1. Thoroughly grease a 2.4 litre Bundt tin with butter. Next, dust the tin with cocoa powder, tapping out any excess but making sure all areas are covered. Set aside.

2. In a medium pan over a low heat, melt the butter, cocoa powder and coffee, whisking occasionally, until the mixture is smooth and combined. Cool for 10min.

3. Meanwhile, in a large bowl, mix together the flour, baking powder, bicarbonate of soda, sugar and a large pinch of fine salt to combine. In a separate jug, whisk together the eggs, yogurt and vanilla until combined.

4. Heat the oven to 180°C (160°C fan) mark 4. Scrape the cooled butter mixture into the flour bowl and whisk until combined. Add the egg mixture and whisk again. Scrape into the prepared tin, then level and bake for 45–50min, or until a skewer inserted into the centre of the cake comes out clean. Leave to cool in the tin for 3min, then invert on to a wire rack, remove the tin and leave to cool completely.

5. When the cake is cool, make the glaze. Heat the cream in a small pan until there are bubbles appearing around the inside edge of the pan. Put the chocolate into a heatproof bowl and pour over the hot cream. Leave for a few minutes, then stir until combined. Mix in the golden syrup, then set aside for 10min to cool and thicken.

6. Transfer the cake to a cake stand or serving plate. Spoon over the warm glaze, encouraging it to drip down the sides, and decorate with chocolate coffee truffles, if you like. Serve in slices.

MOTHER'S DAY

The *Good Housekeeping* cookery team share the special
family bakes that first got them interested in cooking...

Alice's Marmalade and White Chocolate Loaf

'Mum grew up in a bakery, so the house was always full of sweet treats. She makes the most deliciously tangy marmalade, the secret to which, I've learned, is adding less sugar. It pairs perfectly with sweet white chocolate.'
Cookery writer, Alice Shields

175g unsalted butter, softened, plus extra to grease
175g caster sugar
2 medium eggs
75g natural yogurt
1 tsp vanilla bean paste
200g self-raising flour
Finely grated zest ½ orange
75g white chocolate chips, plus extra melted white
   chocolate to drizzle (optional)
100g good-quality marmalade

Hands-on time: 20min, plus cooling
Cooking time: about 1hr 5min
Serves 8

PER SERVING 446cals, 5g protein, 23g fat (14g saturates), 55g carbs (36g total sugars), 1g fibre

◆ TO STORE
Keep in an airtight container at room temperature for up to 5 days.

1. Heat the oven to 170°C (150°C fan) mark 3. Grease and line a 900g loaf tin with baking parchment.

2. In a large bowl, beat the butter and sugar with a handheld electric whisk until pale and fluffy. Add the eggs one at a time, beating well after each addition. Add the yogurt and vanilla and beat until just combined. With a large metal spoon, fold in the flour, orange zest and chocolate chips.

3. Reserve 2 tbsp of the marmalade to glaze and ripple the rest through the batter. Scrape into the prepared tin and level. Bake for 1hr without opening the oven door, until golden brown. Cool completely in the tin.

4. To make the glaze, bubble the reserved marmalade and ½ tbsp water in a small pan over medium-high heat until syrupy. If you want a smooth glaze, pass through a fine sieve. Leave to cool slightly.

5. Transfer the cooled cake to a serving plate or board. Brush over the glaze and drizzle with melted chocolate, if you like. Serve in slices.

Alice and Helen

Meike's Spekkoek

'My father often travelled to Holland with his work, and when he brought back this delicious treat, I was hooked. I remember sneaking thin slivers of this expensive treat with my brother and peeling apart the layers to make the joy last longer!'
Cookery director, Meike Beck

FOR THE SPICE MIX
2 tsp ground cinnamon
1 tsp ground ginger
1 tsp ground cardamom (from about 12 green pods)
½ tsp ground nutmeg
¼ tsp ground cloves

FOR THE CAKE
250g unsalted butter, softened, plus extra to grease
250g caster sugar
8 medium eggs, separated
200g plain flour
Icing sugar, to dust

TO BRUSH
75g unsalted butter, melted

Hands-on time: 50min, plus cooling
Cooking time: about 35min
Serves 20

PER SERVING 234cals, 4g protein, 15g fat (9g saturates), 20g carbs (13g total sugars), trace fibre

◆ TO STORE
This cake keeps well, and gets better with a little age. Keep well-wrapped in clingfilm and store at room temperature for up to 7 days.

1. In a small bowl, combine the spice mix ingredients and set aside. Heat the grill to medium-high. Grease a 20.5cm round springform tin and line the base with baking parchment.

2. For the cake, beat the butter and half the sugar in a large bowl with a handheld electric whisk until pale and fluffy. Gradually beat in the egg yolks, whisking well after each addition. Using a large metal spoon, fold in the flour (the mixture will be fairly stiff).

3. With clean beaters and in a separate bowl, whisk the egg whites until they hold stiff peaks. Gradually beat in the remaining sugar until the meringue is stiff and shiny. Thoroughly mix a large spoonful of the meringue into the butter mixture to loosen it, then fold in the remaining whites in 2 batches. Spoon half the mixture into a separate bowl (weigh for best results) and fold the spice mixture into it.

4. Spread a thin layer of the plain mixture (about 3 tbsp) into the base of the prepared tin, spreading it in to an even layer with the back of a tablespoon. Put under the grill so the top of the cake tin is about 7.5–10cm under the heat. Grill for 1½–3min, or until the cake layer is just cooked and very lightly golden (keep checking it), then brush the cake with melted butter (avoid the sides of the tin). Repeat with more layers, grilling and brushing, alternating the mixtures (you should end up with about 12 layers, but it doesn't matter if there are more or less).

5. Cool completely in the tin. Transfer the spekkoek to a cake stand, dust with icing sugar and serve in thin slices.

Meike and Marianne

Emma and Doreen

Emma's Millionaire's Shortbread

'This recipe was gifted to Mum by an old friend. She then taught it to me, with a few of her adaptations. Growing up near the Maldon coast, which is famed for its sea salt, we were adding salt to sweet treats long before it was fashionable, and it's this along with the black treacle that balance the sweetness of this bake perfectly.'
Cookery editor, Emma Franklin

FOR THE SHORTBREAD BASE
225g unsalted butter, plus extra to grease
275g plain flour
125g caster sugar
Pinch flaked sea salt

FOR THE TOPPING
225g unsalted butter, in small pieces
397g tin condensed milk
175g caster sugar
3 tbsp golden syrup
1 tbsp black treacle
½ tsp vanilla extract
¼ tsp flaked sea salt
225g dark chocolate, roughly chopped

Hands-on time: 40min, plus chilling, cooling and setting
Cooking time: about 35min
Makes 20 squares

PER SQUARE 408cals, 4g protein, 23g fat (15g saturates), 45g carbs (35g total sugars), 1g fibre

◆ TO STORE
Keep in an airtight container in the fridge for up to a week.

◆ EMMA'S TIP
'If, like my dad, you have a very sweet tooth, use a mixture of dark and milk chocolate to make the topping layer.'

1. Heat the oven to 180°C (160°C fan) mark 4. Grease and line the base and sides of a 23 x 33cm tin with baking parchment.

2. To make the base, pulse the butter and flour in a food processor until the mixture resembles fine breadcrumbs. Alternatively, rub the butter into the flour using your fingertips. Pulse/stir in the sugar and salt. Tip the mixture on to a work surface and bring together with your hands. Press into the prepared tin and level as best you can. Prick the base all over with a fork and chill for 15min.

3. Bake the shortbread for 25min until lightly golden, then cool in the tin.

4. Meanwhile, make the caramel topping: put the butter, condensed milk, sugar, syrup and treacle into a pan and stir constantly over a low heat until the butter has melted and the mixture is combined. Increase the heat to medium and bring very slowly to the boil, stirring occasionally, then simmer gently for 8–10min, stirring constantly, until it is a deep caramel colour. Stir in the vanilla and salt, then pour over the shortbread. Leave to set at room temperature for 1hr.

5. Melt the chocolate in a heatproof bowl set over a pan of gently simmering water. Pour over the caramel and spread to level, then chill until set. To serve, transfer to a board and cut into squares.

Grace's Rhubarb and Custard Éclairs

'Such a classic combination, and one that takes me right back to long childhood walks, where Mum would supply us with rhubarb and custard boiled sweets for encouragement.'
Digital cookery writer, Grace Evans

Jane and Grace

FOR THE CHOUX PASTRY
150g unsalted butter, plus extra to grease
200g plain flour
4 medium eggs, beaten

FOR THE CRÈME PÂTISSIÈRE
350ml milk
5 medium egg yolks
75g caster sugar
25g plain flour
2½ tsp cornflour
2 tsp vanilla bean paste

FOR THE RHUBARB
75g caster sugar
250g forced pink rhubarb, trimmed and cut into 2cm
    pieces, halved horizontally

FOR THE ICING
200g icing sugar, sifted
Pink gel food colouring (optional)
A few rhubarb and custard boiled sweets, crushed

Hands-on time: 45min, plus cooling, chilling
    and setting
Cooking time: about 50min
Makes 16 éclairs

PER ÉCLAIR 260cals, 5g protein, 11g fat (6g saturates),
35g carbs (23g total sugars), 1g fibre

1. Heat the oven to 200°C (180°C fan) mark 6.
   Lightly grease and line 2 large baking trays with
   baking parchment. To make the choux pastry,
   melt the butter and 450ml water in a medium
   pan over low heat. Turn up the heat and bring

to the boil. As soon as it boils, take the pan off the
heat and quickly beat in the flour with a wooden
spoon. Keep beating until the mixture is shiny and
comes away from the sides of the pan. Empty into
a large bowl and cool for 10min.

2. Using a handheld electric whisk, gradually beat
   enough egg into the dough until a spoonful of
   it will reluctantly fall off the spoon if held above
   the bowl (too loose and the éclairs won't rise
   well). Scrape into a piping bag fitted with a
   1.25cm plain nozzle. Pipe a 13.5cm line on to
   a lined tray, doubling back so it's 2 lines thick.
   Repeat with the remaining mixture to make
   16 éclairs, spacing them apart. With a damp
   finger, gently pat down any peaks.

3. Bake for 30–35min until deep golden and crisp.
   Remove from the oven (leave the oven on).
   Wearing an oven glove and using a serrated

knife, carefully slice each eclair in half lengthways, leaving each one attached at one end. Return to the oven (opened out) for 5–7min to dry out. Cool on a wire rack.

4. Meanwhile, make the crème pâtissière. Heat the milk in a pan until just steaming. Beat the yolks, sugar, flour, cornflour and vanilla together in a heatproof bowl. Gradually whisk a third of the milk into the egg mixture, until smooth. Whisk the egg mixture back into the remaining milk in the pan and cook over medium heat, whisking constantly until thick and smooth (it will go very lumpy at first). Remove from the heat, scrape into a bowl and lay clingfilm on the surface to stop a skin from forming. Cool, then chill until needed.

5. For the rhubarb, line a large baking tray with fresh baking parchment. Heat the sugar with 200ml water in a medium pan over low heat, stirring to dissolve the sugar. Increase the heat to medium and bubble for 1min. Add the rhubarb and cook gently for 1–2min, until just beginning to soften. Remove the rhubarb to the prepared tray with a slotted spoon. Cool completely.

6. To make the icing, mix the icing sugar with just enough water to make a thick but spreadable icing. Mix in some pink food colouring, if using.

7. Scrape the cooled crème pâtissière into a piping bag fitted with a 1cm star nozzle and pipe a layer of cream into each éclair in a swirl. Arrange the rhubarb on top. Close the éclairs and spread icing on top, then sprinkle over the sweets. Serve immediately.

◆ GET AHEAD
Prepare to end of step 4 up to a day ahead. Store cooled éclairs in an airtight container at room temperature. Up to 1hr before serving, refresh the éclairs on a baking tray in a 200°C (180°C fan) mark 6 oven for 5min, until crisp. Cool. Stir the crème pâtissière before assembling.

Georgie's Coffee, Cardamom and Hazelnut Cake

'Having a coffee cake at every special occasion is a long-standing tradition in my family.'
Cookery assistant, Georgie D'Arcy Coles

Ⓥ

FOR THE CAKE
225g unsalted butter, softened, plus extra to grease
7 green cardamom pods
225g caster sugar
4 medium eggs, beaten
225g self-raising flour
4 tbsp espresso or strong black coffee, cooled
75g chopped roasted hazelnuts

FOR THE COFFEE SYRUP
50ml espresso or strong black coffee
50g caster sugar

FOR THE ICING
150g unsalted butter, softened
200g icing sugar
4 tbsp espresso or strong black coffee, cooled
25g chopped roasted hazelnuts, to decorate

Hands-on time: 35min, plus cooling
Cooking time: about 1hr
Serves 12

PER SERVING 537cals, 6g protein, 33g fat (17g saturates), 54g carbs (40g total sugars), 1g fibre

◆ TO STORE
Keep in an airtight container at room temperature for up to 2 days.

1. Heat the oven to 180°C (160°C fan) mark 4. Lightly grease a deep 20.5cm round loose-bottomed cake tin and line with baking parchment. For the cake, use a pestle and mortar to bash the cardamom pods to break the husks. Pick out the black seeds and discard the husks. Grind the seeds until fine.

2. Using a freestanding mixer or handheld electric whisk, beat the butter and sugar until pale and fluffy. Gradually beat in the eggs (if the mixture looks as if it's curdling, mix in a few tbsp of the flour). Whisk in the espresso/coffee.

3. Sift in the flour, add the ground cardamom and hazelnuts and fold in with a large metal spoon. Scrape into the prepared tin, level gently and bake for between 55min and 1hr, or until a skewer inserted into the centre comes out clean. Cool in the tin for 5min, then transfer to a cooling rack to cool completely.

4. Meanwhile, make the coffee syrup. Heat the espresso/coffee, sugar and 50ml water in a small pan over a low heat, stirring until the sugar dissolves. Increase the heat and bubble until syrupy, about 5min. Set aside to cool.

5. For the icing, beat the butter using a freestanding mixer or handheld electric whisk, until pale and fluffy. Sift in the icing sugar and whisk on low speed until combined. Add the espresso/coffee and mix to combine.

6. Cut the cooled cake in half horizontally. Use a third of the icing to sandwich the halves back together and set the cake on a cake stand or serving plate. Spread the remaining icing over the top, drizzle over the coffee syrup and scatter over the roasted hazelnuts. Serve in slices.

◆ GEORGIE'S TIP
'If you're baking for kids, replace the espresso with Camp Chicory & Coffee Essence like my mum did. You will only need 1 tsp extract for every 1 tbsp espresso.'

Susie and Georgie

8

Free From

Wheat-free Lemon and Blueberry Polenta Cake

A pretty choice for an afternoon tea or bake sale. If you have some limoncello, you could add a dash of it to the icing for extra kick.

FOR THE CAKE
225g unsalted butter, very soft
225g caster sugar
4 medium eggs, lightly beaten
Zest and juice 2 lemons (keep zest and juice separate)
75g quick-cook polenta
150g gluten-free plain flour (we used Doves Farm Plain White Flour Blend)
1½ tsp gluten-free baking powder
200g blueberries

TO DECORATE
300ml double cream
4 tbsp icing sugar, sifted
4 tbsp lemon curd
100g blueberries
Pared lemon zest (optional)

Hands-on time: 20min, plus cooling
Cooking time: about 40min
Serves 16

PER SERVING 353cals, 3g protein, 23g fat (14g saturates), 33g carbs (22g total sugars), 1g fibre

◆ TO STORE
Keep the cake in an airtight container in the fridge for up to 3 days. Allow it to come up to room temperature before serving.

1. Heat the oven to 180°C (160°C fan) mark 4 and line a roasting tin roughly 20.5cm x 30.5cm x 5cm with baking parchment.

2. To make the cake, put the butter and sugar into a large bowl and beat with a handheld electric whisk until light and fluffy, about 3min. Gradually add the eggs, whisking well after each addition. Whisk in the lemon zest.

3. Use a large metal spoon to fold in the polenta, gluten-free flour, baking powder and 2 tbsp of lemon juice to make a smooth batter. Carefully fold in half of the blueberries. Spoon the mixture into the prepared tin and level the surface. Scatter over the remaining blueberries.

4. Bake for 40min or until golden and a skewer inserted into the centre comes out clean. Cool in the tin for 5min, then lift out and cool in its parchment on a wire rack.

5. Once the cake is completely cool, peel off the parchment and transfer the cake to a large serving plate or board. To decorate, put the cream and icing sugar into a bowl and whip until the mixture holds soft peaks, then quickly whip in the lemon curd.

6. Spread the icing on top of the cooled cake and scatter over the 100g blueberries and pared lemon zest, if using. Cut into squares to serve.

Dairy and Gluten-free Passion Loaf with Pistachio Crumb

If you prefer, you can use plain flour and butter instead of gluten-free flour and dairy-free spread.

150ml sunflower oil, plus extra to grease
3 medium eggs
150g light brown soft sugar
175g gluten-free self-raising flour
1 tsp gluten-free bicarbonate of soda
1 tsp ground cinnamon
1 tsp ground mixed spice
150g carrots, coarsely grated
227g tin pineapple slices in juice, drained and
    roughly chopped
50g pistachios, roughly chopped

FOR THE CRUMBLE TOPPING
40g dairy-free spread
40g gluten-free self-raising flour
40g demerara sugar
50g pistachios, roughly chopped

Hands-on time: 20min, plus cooling
Cooking time: about 1hr 10min
Cuts into 8 slices

PER SLICE 466cals, 8g protein, 26g fat (4g saturates), 48g carbs (27g total sugars), 3g fibre

◆ TO STORE
Keep in an airtight container at room temperature for up to 3 days.

1. Heat the oven to 180°C (160°C fan) mark 4. Grease and line a 900g loaf tin with baking parchment.

2. For the crumble topping, rub the spread and flour together until it resembles large breadcrumbs. Stir in the demerara sugar and pistachios.

3. In a jug, whisk together the oil and eggs. In a large bowl, combine the sugar, flour, bicarbonate of soda and spices. Add the oil mixture to the dry ingredients, stirring well. Stir in the carrots, pineapple and pistachios, then scrape the batter into the tin. Level and sprinkle over the crumble topping.

4. Bake for 60–70min, or until a skewer inserted into the centre comes out clean. Cool for 5min in the tin, then transfer to a wire rack to cool completely. Serve in slices.

Gluten-free Cherry Bakewell Loaf

This almond-flavoured cake is the perfect teatime treat. In season, use pitted fresh cherries in place of glacé cherries.

250g unsalted butter, softened, plus extra to grease
250g caster sugar
4 large eggs
½ tsp almond extract
150g gluten-free self-raising flour
75g ground almonds

FOR THE STREUSEL
50g unsalted butter, melted
50g light brown soft sugar
75g gluten-free self-raising flour
25g flaked almonds
200g glacé cherries, washed and dried

FOR THE ICING
175g icing sugar
1 tbsp flaked almonds, toasted (optional)

Hands-on time: 20min, plus cooling and setting
Cooking time: about 1hr 15min
Cuts into 10 slices

**PER SLICE 650cals, 8g protein, 34g fat (17g saturates),
77g carbs (61g total sugars), 2g fibre**

◆ TO STORE
The iced loaf will keep in an airtight container
at room temperature for up to 3 days.

1. Heat the oven to 180°C (160°C fan) mark 4. Grease and line the base and sides of a 900g loaf tin with baking parchment, allowing the parchment to come 5cm above the top of the tin. For the cake, in a large bowl beat the butter and sugar with a handheld electric whisk until light and fluffy – it takes about 5min.

2. In a small jug, beat the eggs with the almond extract. Add the egg mixture, flour and ground almonds to the butter mixture and whisk until smooth. Spoon into the prepared tin, level the surface and bake for an initial 55min.

3. Meanwhile, make the streusel: mix together the butter, sugar, flour and almonds. After 55min, remove the tin from the oven and carefully sprinkle over the streusel mixture in large clumps, then scatter over the cherries. Return the tin to the oven for 15–20min until a skewer inserted into the centre comes out clean. Cool in the tin on a wire rack.

4. When the cake is cool, remove from the tin and peel off the parchment. To make the icing, mix the icing sugar with 1½ tbsp water to make a thick icing (you may need a drop more water). Pipe or spoon the icing over the loaf, sprinkle over the almonds (if using) and allow to set before serving in slices.

Pistachio and Raspberry Upside-down Cake

Made with pistachios, almonds and polenta for texture, this gluten-free cake is beautifully moist.

250g unsalted butter, softened, plus extra to grease
125g pistachios
250g caster sugar
4 medium eggs, at room temperature
100g ground almonds
100g quick-cook polenta
½ tsp each vanilla and almond extract
Finely grated zest 1 orange
2 tsp gluten-free baking powder
125g raspberries

TO DECORATE (optional)
25g pistachios, roughly chopped
Small handful raspberries
Crème fraîche

Hands-on time: 15min, plus cooling
Cooking time: about 55min
Serves 12

PER SERVING 425cals, 8g protein, 31g fat (13g saturates), 29g carbs (22g total sugars), 2g fibre

◆ GET AHEAD
Make up to a day ahead, cool completely, then store in an airtight container. Leftover cake will keep for up to 3 days.

1. Heat the oven to 180°C (160°C fan) mark 4. Lightly grease and line a 23cm round springform cake tin with baking parchment.

2. Whizz the pistachios in a food processor until finely ground (or bash in a food bag with a rolling pin). In a large bowl, beat together the butter and sugar using a handheld electric whisk until very pale and fluffy, about 5min. Crack in the eggs one at a time, whisking well after each addition. With the motor on slow speed, mix in the ground pistachios and almonds, polenta, vanilla and almond extracts, orange zest, baking powder and a pinch of fine salt until combined. Fold in half of the raspberries.

3. Scatter the remaining raspberries into the base of the prepared tin, then spoon over the cake mixture and level. Bake for about 50–55min or until risen and golden (cover with foil for the final 15min if getting too dark).

4. Cool in the tin for 15min, then remove and transfer to a wire rack to cool completely.

5. To serve, invert on to a serving plate or board and peel off the baking parchment. Scatter over chopped pistachios and raspberries, and serve with crème fraîche, if you like.

Vegan Chocolate Cake

Fluffy and decadent, this recipe is the only one you'll need if you're looking for a celebration cake without eggs or dairy. While most baking powders are suitable for vegans, do check the brand to be sure.

FOR THE CAKE
125ml vegetable oil, plus extra to grease
175g caster sugar
250g plain flour
50g dairy-free raw cacao powder
1 tsp bicarbonate of soda
1½ tsp baking powder
2 tsp vanilla extract
1½ tbsp cider vinegar
300ml dairy-free milk alternative, we used oat milk

FOR THE ICING
150g dairy-free dark chocolate, chopped, plus extra,
    grated, to decorate
150g dairy-free sunflower spread, chilled
150g baking block, softened
250g icing sugar, sifted
50g dairy-free raw cacao powder

Hands-on time: 25min, plus cooling
Cooking time: about 50min
Serves 12

**PER SERVING 543cals, 5g protein, 29g fat (8g
saturates), 63g carbs (44g total sugars), 4g fibre**

◆ TO STORE
Loosely cover and keep at room temperature
for up to 3 days.

1. Heat the oven to 180°C (160°C fan) mark 4. Grease and line a 20.5cm round cake tin with baking parchment. For the cake, sift the sugar, flour, cacao, bicarbonate of soda and baking powder into a large bowl.

2. In a separate jug, mix the oil, vanilla, vinegar and milk alternative. Pour the wet ingredients on to the dry ones and whisk to mix. Pour into the prepared tin and bake for 45min or until risen and a skewer inserted into the centre comes out clean. Leave the cake to cool for 5min in the tin, then transfer to a wire rack to cool completely.

3. To make the icing, melt chocolate in a heatproof bowl set over a pan of gently simmering water. Set aside until completely cool but still melted.

4. In a large bowl, beat together the sunflower spread and baking block using a handheld electric whisk, until smooth and combined. Add the icing sugar and cacao powder and beat (starting slowly) until combined. Beat in the cooled chocolate until combined.

5. Split the cooled cake in half horizontally and sandwich back together with some of the icing. Spread remaining icing over the top and sides of cake. Decorate with grated chocolate and serve.

Vegan Spiced Carrot Cake

This cake is so soft, you wouldn't know it was vegan.
We've used wholemeal flour in the mixture and reduced
the refined sugar content for extra goodness.

150g vegan spread, plus extra to grease
250g pitted dates
350ml unsweetened almond milk
2 tsp bicarbonate of soda
75g light brown sugar
Zest and juice 1 orange
350g wholemeal plain flour
1 tbsp baking powder
1½ tsp ground ginger
2 tsp ground cinnamon
250g carrots (peeled weight), coarsely grated
50g desiccated coconut
50g dried cranberries, plus extra to decorate
25g pumpkin seeds, plus extra, toasted, to decorate
50g pecans, chopped, plus extra to decorate

FOR THE ICING
150g vegan spread
75g smooth almond butter
325g icing sugar, sifted

Hands-on time: 35min, plus cooling and chilling
Cooking time: about 50min
Makes 20 squares

PER SQUARE 352cals, 4.5g protein, 17g fat (4g
saturates), 44g carbs (32g total sugars), 4g fibre

1. Heat the oven to 180°C (160°C fan) mark 4.
   Grease and line a 30.5 x 23cm rectangular tin
   with baking parchment.

2. Put the dates and almond milk in a small pan,
   bring up to the boil, then simmer for 5min.
   Transfer to a blender or food processor and
   whizz until smooth. Stir in the bicarbonate
   of soda and set aside.

3. Meanwhile, in a large bowl, beat together the
   vegan spread and sugar with a handheld electric
   whisk until combined. Beat in the date mixture
   along with the orange juice and zest.

4. In a separate bowl, mix together the flour,
   baking powder and spices. Fold into the batter,
   followed by the carrots, coconut, cranberries,
   pumpkin seeds and pecans.

5. Transfer to the roasting tin and spread to level.
   Bake for 45–50min, until a skewer inserted in
   the centre comes out clean. Cool in the tin on
   a wire rack.

6. Meanwhile, make the icing. In a medium
   bowl, beat the spread and almond butter with a
   handheld electric whisk until smooth. Gradually
   beat in the icing sugar and chill in the fridge
   until needed.

7. Remove the cake from the tin, transfer to
   a board and spread over the icing. Scatter
   with cranberries, pumpkin seeds and pecans.
   Cut into squares to serve.

Vegan Banoffee Pie

A sweet treat that's too good to resist. The pillowy topping works so well with the toffee layer and crunchy base.

FOR THE BASE
200g Lotus Biscoff biscuits
2 tbsp coconut oil, melted
1 tbsp agave syrup

FOR THE FILLING
500ml coconut cream
150g light brown soft sugar

FOR THE TOPPING
175g dairy-free coconut yogurt
100g coconut cream
2 tbsp icing sugar, sifted
2 bananas, cut into 1cm thick slices
Vegan cocoa powder, to dust

Hands-on time: 25min, plus cooling and chilling
Cooking time: about 30min
Serves 10

PER SERVING 362cals, 2g protein, 21g fat (17g saturates), 42g carbs (32g total sugars), 1g fibre

◆ GET AHEAD
Make the pie up to the end of step 3 up to 4hr ahead. Complete the recipe to serve.

1. Heat the oven to 180°C (160°C fan) mark 4 and line the base of a 20.5cm round, loose-bottomed, fluted tart tin with baking parchment. Whizz the biscuits to crumbs in a food processor or put in a food bag and bash with a rolling pin. Pulse/ mix in the melted coconut oil and agave syrup. Tip into the lined tin and press into the base and 2.5cm up the sides of the tin with the back of a spoon (making sure the sides aren't too thin). Bake for 10min, then set aside to cool.

2. For the filling, heat the coconut cream and sugar in a medium pan over medium heat, stirring to dissolve the sugar. Bring to the boil, then bubble for 15–18min, stirring frequently, until thickened and a deep caramel colour. Pour into the biscuit base; cool and chill for 1hr.

3. Meanwhile, to make the topping, whisk together the dairy-free coconut yogurt, the coconut cream and icing sugar until combined. Chill until needed.

4. To serve, transfer the pie to a cake stand or plate. Arrange the bananas on the filling, spoon on the topping and dust with the cocoa powder.

Wheat-free Hazelnut and Raspberry Meringue Cake

An impressive yet easy-to-make dessert that can be prepared ahead of time and frozen.

5 medium egg whites
275g caster sugar
75g hazelnuts, roasted and finely chopped
300ml double cream
2 tbsp icing sugar, sifted
75-100g frozen raspberries, defrosted
40g dark chocolate (70% cocoa solids), melted

Hands-on time: 25min, plus cooling
Cooking time: about 40min
Serves 8

PER SERVING 440cals, 5g protein, 28g fat (14g saturates), 43g carbs (43g total sugars), 1g fibre

◆ FREEZE AHEAD
Prepare to end of step 3 up to one month ahead. Put both meringues on one baking sheet. Wrap in clingfilm and freeze. To serve, defrost completely, then complete the recipe.

1. Heat the oven to 160°C (140°C fan) mark 3. Line 2 baking sheets with baking parchment and draw a 20.5cm circle on each sheet. Flip the parchment over so the ink is on the bottom.

2. Whisk the egg whites in a large bowl until stiff but not dry. Gradually add the caster sugar, mixing well after each addition, until thick and glossy. Quickly beat in the hazelnuts.

3. Divide the meringue mixture equally between the prepared baking sheets and smooth into a circle inside the marked lines. Bake for 30–40min until lightly golden and easy to peel away from the paper. Leave to cool completely on the baking sheet – the meringues may crack slightly.

4. Pour the cream into a bowl. Add the icing sugar and whisk until the mixture just holds its shape. Tip in the raspberries and lightly whisk to break up the fruit.

5. Put one of the meringue discs on a serving plate. Cover with the raspberry cream and top with the remaining meringue disc. Use a teaspoon to drizzle over melted chocolate and serve.

Gluten-free Chocolate Orange Cheesecake

This creamy treat, pictured on page 215, can be prepared and frozen up to one month in advance.

FOR THE BASE
50g butter, melted
200g gluten-free dark chocolate digestives, finely crushed

FOR THE FILLING
500g cream cheese
150ml soured cream
200g caster sugar
1½ tbsp gluten-free plain flour
1 tsp vanilla extract
Zest 1 orange
2 medium eggs, separated

TO DECORATE
150g dark chocolate (70% cocoa solids)

Hands-on time: 20min, plus chilling
Cooking time: about 40min
Serves 8

PER SERVING 592cals, 8g protein, 37g fat (22g saturates), 56g carbs (45g total sugars), 1g fibre

◆ FREEZE AHEAD
Prepare to end of step 3 up to one month in advance. Wrap the tin in clingfilm and freeze. To serve, defrost completely in the fridge and complete the recipe.

1. Grease a 20.5cm springform tin. Mix the butter and crushed biscuits and press into the base. Chill for 15min.

2. Heat the oven to 180°C (160°C fan) mark 4. In a large bowl, whisk together all the filling ingredients, except egg whites, until smooth. Whisk the egg whites in a separate bowl until they reach soft peak stage. Use a large metal spoon to mix a spoonful of egg whites into the cream cheese mixture to loosen, then fold in the remaining egg whites.

3. Pour the mixture into the tin and level. Bake for 35–40min until lightly golden – the filling will firm up on chilling. Leave to cool – it may crack on top, but this will be covered by decoration. Chill for 2hr or overnight.

4. Melt the chocolate and pour on to a baking sheet. Chill for 10min until just set but not solid. Pull a large knife towards you across the chocolate to make a curl. Repeat until you've made enough curls to cover the cheesecake. Take the cheesecake out of the tin and transfer to a serving plate. Scatter over the chocolate curls and serve in slices.

Flourless Chocolate and Chestnut Torte

Earthy chestnuts and rich chocolate combine to make a delicious, dense pudding cake.

200g unsalted butter, chopped, plus extra to grease
100g cooked chestnuts
200g caster sugar
200g dark chocolate (70% cocoa solids), chopped
200g ground almonds
6 medium eggs, separated

TO DECORATE
300ml double cream
1 tsp vanilla bean paste
1 tbsp icing sugar, sifted
1 tsp cocoa powder, to dust

Hands-on time: 30min, plus cooling
Cooking time: about 45min
Cuts into 12 slices

PER SLICE 563cals, 9g protein, 44g fat (21g saturates), 32g carbs (30g total sugars), 2g fibre

◆ GET AHEAD
Prepare to end of step 4 up to a day ahead. Store the cooled cake in an airtight container at room temperature. Complete recipe to serve.

1. Heat the oven to 180°C (160°C fan) mark 4. Grease and line a 23cm round springform tin with baking parchment.

2. In a food processor, whizz the chestnuts and 25g of the sugar to a smooth paste. Set aside. Melt the butter and chocolate in a large pan over a low heat. Cool slightly before stirring through the chestnut mixture and ground almonds.

3. Beat the remaining sugar and egg yolks in a large bowl with a handheld electric whisk until pale and fluffy – about 5min. Add the chocolate mixture and fold in with a large metal spoon.

4. Using clean beaters and a separate bowl, beat the egg whites to stiff peaks. Fold the whites through the chocolate mixture. Scrape into the lined tin, level gently and bake for 40min, or until cake has risen and is firm to the touch. Leave to cool completely in the tin.

5. To serve, whip the cream, vanilla and icing sugar to soft peaks with a handheld electric whisk. Transfer the cake to a cake stand or plate and peel off the baking parchment. Spoon on the cream, dust with cocoa and serve in slices.

Vegan Choc-chip Cookies

These easy biscuits are delicious served warm.

250g plain flour
100g light brown soft sugar
100g caster sugar
½ tsp baking powder
½ tsp bicarbonate of soda
1 tsp vanilla extract
125g coconut oil, melted
50ml almond milk
2 tbsp almond butter
150g vegan dark chocolate (70% cocoa solids), chopped
   into chunks

Hands-on time: 20min, plus cooling
Cooking time: about 15min
Makes 12 cookies

PER COOKIE 318cals, 3g protein, 16g fat (11g saturates), 40g carbs, (24g total sugars), 2g fibre

◆ TO STORE
Keep in an airtight container at room temperature for up to 4 days.

1. Heat the oven to 180°C (160°C fan) mark 4. In a large bowl, mix the flour, sugars, baking powder and bicarbonate of soda with ½ tsp fine salt. In a separate bowl, mix the vanilla extract, coconut oil, almond milk and almond butter.

2. Stir the wet ingredients into the dry ingredients until combined. Stir through the chocolate chunks. Set aside.

3. Line 2 baking sheets with baking parchment. Roll the cookie dough into 12 equal balls using your hands. Space apart on the prepared sheets, as they'll spread when baking. Bake for 10–15min, until lightly golden. Allow to cool on trays for 5min before transferring to a cooling rack. Serve warm or at room temperature.

Leek and Bacon Quiche

There's no gluten in this pastry so it can't be overworked, which means you'll get a crumbly texture no matter how much you handle it.

125g cold unsalted butter, cubed
250g gluten-free plain flour
1 medium egg, beaten
2 leeks, sliced
1 tbsp sunflower oil
300g smoked bacon lardons
1 garlic clove, crushed
2 sprigs thyme, leaves picked
4 large eggs
300ml double cream
200ml crème fraiche
100g Cheddar cheese, grated

Hands-on time: 20min, plus chilling and cooling
Cooking time: about 1hr
Serves 8

PER SERVING 729cals, 18g protein, 61g fat (35g saturates), 25g carbs (2g total sugars), 2g fibre

1. In a large bowl, rub together the butter, gluten-free plain flour and 1 tsp salt until the mixture resembles breadcrumbs. Stir in the beaten egg and 1 tsp cold water, then knead well until smooth.

2. Roll out the pastry on a lightly floured surface, then use to line a 23cm loose-bottomed tart tin that's at least 4cm deep. Don't worry if you need to patch the pastry in places. Chill for 30min.

3. Heat the oven to 190°C (170°C fan), mark 5. Line the pastry with greaseproof paper, fill with baking beans and blind bake for 15–20min. Remove the beans and paper, then bake for 5min until sandy to the touch. Set aside.

4. Meanwhile, gently fry the leeks in the sunflower oil for 5min, then add the bacon lardons and fry for 5min more. Stir through the crushed garlic and thyme leaves.

5. In a jug, beat together the eggs, cream, crème fraîche, Cheddar cheese and plenty of seasoning. Spoon the leek and bacon mixture into the pastry case, then pour in the egg mixture. Bake the quiche for 30–35min, or until golden and just set. Leave to cool for 5–10min. Serve.

Wheatless Brown Loaf

This unusual bread recipe is made with a batter rather than a kneaded dough. Because it's so wet, it only needs one rise. It doesn't have a heavy chew, but it makes the perfect sandwich loaf.

250ml milk
10g fast-action dried yeast
1 tbsp granulated sugar
75ml vegetable oil, plus extra to grease
600g gluten-free brown bread flour
½ tsp cream of tartar
½ tbsp white wine vinegar
2 medium eggs

Hands-on time: 15min, plus rising and cooling
Cooking time: about 40min
Cuts into 12 slices

PER SLICE 238cals, 5g protein, 6g fat (1g saturates), 39g carbs (2g total sugars), 2g fibre

◆ TO STORE
Once cool, wrap well in clingfilm and keep at room temperature for up to 3 days.

1. Heat the milk and 100ml water until just warm (not hot). Mix in the yeast and sugar and set aside for 5min, until foaming. Lightly grease and line a 900g loaf tin with baking parchment.

2. Meanwhile, using a freestanding mixer fitted with a paddle attachment, mix the gluten-free bread flour, cream of tartar and 1½ tsp fine salt to combine. Alternatively, do this by hand using a wooden spoon.

3. Add the vinegar, eggs, oil and the milk mixture and beat for 1min to combine. Scrape into the prepared tin and smooth to level (the tin will be full). Cover with greased clingfilm (oil-side down) and leave to rise in a warm place for 1½hr, until well risen above the top of the tin.

4. Heat the oven to 180°C (160°C fan) mark 4. Once risen, bake for 30min, then carefully remove the loaf from the tin. Set on a baking tray and return to the oven for 10min, until the sides are golden and crisp. Cool completely on a wire rack before slicing.

9

Pies & Tarts

Autumn Fruit Pie

We used autumn leaf cutters for our decorations, but any 5cm cutters will work for this pretty pastry top.

FOR THE PASTRY
250g plain flour, plus extra to dust
150g unsalted butter, chilled and diced
3 tbsp caster sugar
1 medium egg, separated
2 tsp cider vinegar

FOR THE FILLING
2 ripe pears, peeled and cut into 4cm chunks
3 eating apples, peeled and cut into 4cm chunks
3 tbsp demerara sugar
1 tsp vanilla extract
1 tsp mixed spice
3 ripe plums, destoned and cut into 2.5cm chunks
3 tbsp damson, plum or blackberry jam
50g ground almonds
1 tbsp cornflour

Hands-on time: 50min, plus chilling and cooling
Cooking time: about 45min
Serves 8

PER SERVING (without cream/custard) 423cals,
6g protein, 20g fat (10g saturates), 52g carbs
(28g total sugars), 4g fibre

1. In a food processor, pulse the flour and butter until the mixture resembles fine breadcrumbs. Alternatively, rub the butter into the flour with your fingers. Pulse or stir in the caster sugar. In a small jug, mix the egg yolk and vinegar with 2 tbsp ice-cold water. Add nearly all of it to the flour mixture and pulse or mix in with a cutlery knife until the pastry comes together. If it looks dry, pulse or mix in the remaining yolk mixture. Tip on to a work surface and bring pastry together. Break off a third of the pastry, then shape both portions into flat discs and wrap each in clingfilm. Chill for 30min.

2. On a lightly floured surface, roll out the larger pastry disc and use to line a 23cm fluted tart tin. Trim overhanging pastry with a sharp knife, then wrap trimmings in clingfilm. Chill the lined tin and trimmings for 20min.

3. Meanwhile, mix the pears and apples in a medium bowl with the demerara sugar, vanilla and mixed spice. Set aside for 15min until the fruit releases some of its juices. Mix the plums and jam in a separate bowl, then set aside.

4. On a lightly floured surface, roll out the smaller portion of pastry until 3mm thick. Use cutters to stamp out autumn leaf shapes. Re-roll the trimmings to cut more leaf shapes until all the pastry is used.

5. To assemble the pie, scatter ground almonds into the base of the pastry case. Stir the cornflour through the apples and pears, then spoon the mixture and any juices into the chilled pastry case. Dot over the plums.

6. Starting at the edges of the pie and using the egg white as glue, position the pastry leaves on the pie, overlapping them slightly but leaving space so the fruit below can show through. Chill for 10min.

7. Heat the oven to 190°C (170°C fan) mark 5 and put in a baking sheet to heat up. Brush the pastry leaves with egg white.

8. Bake the pie on the preheated sheet for 45min or until golden. Cool for 5min before removing from the tin. Serve warm or at room temperature with sweetened cream or custard, if you like.

Rhubarb Meringue Pie

The biscuits in the pastry add a subtle, gingery warmth and help to keep the pie case crisp.

FOR THE CURD
400g rhubarb, cut into short lengths
175g caster sugar
Juice ½ orange
2½ tbsp cornflour
3 medium egg yolks
25g unsalted butter, chilled and diced
A little pink gel food colouring (optional)

FOR THE PASTRY
4 gingernut biscuits
225g plain flour, plus extra to dust
125g unsalted butter, chilled and diced
1 medium egg yolk

FOR THE MERINGUE
4 medium egg whites
225g caster sugar
2 tsp cornflour

**Hands-on time: 40min, plus chilling and cooling
Cooking time: about 1hr 15min
Serves 8**

PER SERVING 533cals, 7g protein, 20g fat (11g saturates), 81g carbs (52g total sugars), 2g fibre

1. Heat the oven to 190°C (170°C fan) mark 5. For the curd, mix the rhubarb, 50g of the sugar and 3 tbsp orange juice in a small roasting tin. Cover with foil and roast for 25min or until very tender. Whizz with a stick blender or in a mini food processor until smooth.

2. Meanwhile, make the pastry. Whizz the biscuits to crumbs in a food processor (or bash in a food bag with a rolling pin, then empty into a bowl). Add the flour and pulse/mix to combine. Add the butter and pulse/rub in with fingers until the mixture resembles coarse breadcrumbs. Add the yolk and 2½–3½ tbsp cold water and pulse/mix until the dough comes together. Empty on to a work surface, shape into a disc and wrap in clingfilm. Chill for 10min.

3. On a lightly floured work surface, roll out the dough and use it to line a 23cm loose-bottomed fluted tart tin. Trim the overhang with a sharp knife, then prick the base all over with a fork and chill again for 1hr until firm.

4. Set the tin on a baking tray. Line the pastry case with baking parchment and fill with baking beans. Blind bake for 20min, then remove the parchment and beans and return to the oven for 5–7min until the pastry is pale golden and feels sandy to the touch. Set aside.

5. Meanwhile, finish the curd. In a medium pan, mix together the rhubarb purée, cornflour, egg yolks and remaining 125g sugar. Add the butter. Cook over a low heat, stirring constantly, until thickened (the mixture will need to boil). Remove from the heat and whisk in a little pink food colouring, if using (see GH Tip). Scrape into the baked pastry case, level and chill for 30min.

6. In a clean bowl, whisk the egg whites to stiff peaks with a handheld electric whisk. Combine the sugar and cornflour in a bowl, then add gradually to the whites, whisking well after each addition – the meringue should be stiff and glossy. Spoon on to the rhubarb layer. Bake for 20min until lightly golden. Allow to cool for 20min before serving in slices with cold cream, if you like.

◆ GET AHEAD
Blind bake the pastry case up to a day ahead.
Cool, cover and store at room temperature.
Complete recipe to serve.

◆ GH TIP
The colour of rhubarb varies throughout the
season. A little food colouring helps to give a
vibrant hue if your rhubarb isn't pink enough.

Classic Cherry Pie

Double-crusted pies often have a slightly softer pastry base, but cooking them in the oven on a preheated baking sheet helps to minimise this problem.

FOR THE PASTRY
275g plain flour, plus extra to dust
1 tsp ground cinnamon
40g quick-cook polenta
200g unsalted butter, chilled and cut into cubes
100g caster sugar, plus extra to sprinkle
1 medium egg, lightly beaten

FOR THE FILLING
4 x 425g tins black cherries in syrup
2 tbsp arrowroot
3 tbsp cherry jam
75g caster sugar
1 tbsp kirsch (optional)

Hands-on time: 30min, plus chilling and cooling
Cooking time: about 35min
Serves 8

PER SERVING 503cals, 5g protein, 22g fat (13g saturates), 70g carbs (36g total sugars), 2g fibre

◆ GET AHEAD
Make, wrap and chill the pastry up to a day ahead. Complete the recipe to serve.

1. To make the pastry, put the flour, cinnamon, polenta, butter and a pinch of salt into a food processor. Pulse until the mixture resembles fine breadcrumbs. Alternatively, rub the butter into the flour mixture using your fingers. Add the sugar and pulse/mix briefly, then pulse in 3–4 tbsp ice-cold water (or mix in with a blunt-ended cutlery knife) until the pastry just comes together. Tip on to a work surface, bring together into a flat disc and wrap in clingfilm. Chill for 1hr.

2. Meanwhile, drain the cherries through a sieve set over a jug or bowl. Measure out 150ml of the cherry syrup, then allow the cherries to continue to drain until needed.

3. For the filling, put the arrowroot into a large pan and gradually whisk in the reserved cherry syrup. Next stir in the jam, sugar and kirsch, if using. Heat, whisking frequently, over a medium hob heat until the sauce thickens considerably (it will need to boil) – it will be oddly elastic and stretchy.

4. Give the sieve holding the cherries a good shake, discard any remaining syrup and gently mix the cherries into the sauce. Set aside.

5. Heat the oven to 220°C (200°C fan) mark 7 and put a baking sheet on the middle shelf to heat up. Roll out two-thirds of the pastry on a work surface lightly dusted with flour, then use it to line the base and sides of a 23cm pie tin. Empty in the cooled cherry mixture and level the surface.

6. Roll out the remaining pastry as before until 3mm thick. Lightly brush with beaten egg and sprinkle well with caster sugar. Cut into 2cm wide strips and use these to create a lattice effect on top of the cherries, pressing the strips down well against the edge of the bottom crust to secure them. Trim the edge of the tin to neaten, if necessary.

7. Put the pie on top of the heated baking sheet and bake for 30min or until the pastry is crisp and golden. Allow to cool for at least 10min before serving with cream.

Pecan Pumpkin Pie

With tinned pumpkin purée widely available, this
American classic is now easier than ever to make.

Ⓥ

Plain flour, to dust
375g shortcrust pastry
425g tin 100% pure pumpkin pureé
2 medium eggs, lightly beaten
100ml double cream
1 tsp mixed spice
¼ tsp ground allspice
Pinch ground cloves
200g light soft brown sugar
50g runny honey
100g pecans, chopped

Hands-on time: 20min, plus chilling and cooling
Cooking time: 1hr 25min
Serves 8

PER SERVING 522cals, 7g protein, 31g fat (11g
saturates), 51g carbs (32g total sugars), 4g fibre

1. Heat the oven to 200°C (180°C fan) mark 6.
   Lightly dust a work surface with flour and roll
   out the pastry until it is 5mm thick. Use to line
   a 20.5cm round, 4cm deep fluted tart tin. Set
   the tin on a baking tray and chill for 15min.

2. Line the pastry with a sheet of baking
   parchment and fill with baking beans. Bake for
   15–20min, then carefully remove the beans and
   parchment. Return the tin to the oven and cook
   for a further 10–15min until golden and the base
   feels sandy to the touch. Take out of the oven
   and set aside. Turn down the oven temperature
   to 160°C (140°C fan) mark 3.

3. To make the filling, beat together the pumpkin
   purée, eggs, cream, spices and 175g of the sugar.
   Pour into the cooked pastry case. Bake for 45min,
   or until the filling is just set. Remove from the
   oven and allow to cool completely in the tin.

4. For the pecan topping, line a baking sheet with
   baking parchment. Put the remaining 25g sugar
   and honey in a pan set over a medium heat and
   stir until dissolved. Turn up the heat and boil for
   a few minutes, then add the pecans and stir to
   coat. Tip the pecans on to the paper and set aside
   to cool. Scatter the pecans over the top of the
   tart and serve in slices with cream or ice cream.

Rhubarb Galette

No need to line a tin with this recipe – the beauty of making a free-form tart is that it is meant to look rustic.

FOR THE PASTRY
250g plain flour, plus extra to dust
100g caster sugar, plus 3 tbsp extra
150g unsalted butter, chilled and cut into small pieces
1 large egg yolk

FOR THE FILLING
700g rhubarb, sliced into 2cm diagonal slices
1 tbsp vanilla extract
3 tbsp semolina
1 medium egg, beaten
2 tbsp demerara sugar
Custard, to serve

Hands-on time: 1hr, plus chilling
Cooking time: about 45min
Serves 8

PER SERVING 344cals, 6g protein, 15g fat (7g saturates), 46g carbs (16g total sugars), 3g fibre

1. In a food processor, pulse the flour, 3 tbsp sugar, butter and a large pinch of fine salt until the mixture resembles breadcrumbs. Or combine the ingredients together using a table knife until it forms pea-sized lumps, then continue to rub the mixture together with your fingertips until it resembles breadcrumbs. In a jug, beat together the egg yolk with 3 tbsp ice-cold water. Then gradually add to the flour mixture, stirring it in quickly by hand or with the food processor motor running, until the mixture just comes together into large flakes without becoming sticky. Turn out the pastry on to a lightly floured surface and gently bring together with your hands, kneading briefly. Flatten to form a disc shape, then wrap in clingfilm and chill for 30min.

2. In a large bowl, mix the rhubarb with the remaining 100g sugar and set aside for 1hr, stirring occasionally until the juices are released from the fruit. Use a slotted spoon to lift the rhubarb out of the juice into another large mixing bowl and stir through the vanilla extract. Set the juice aside for later.

3. Heat the oven to 180°C (160°C fan) mark 4 with a flat baking tray inside to preheat. Lightly flour the work surface and a rolling pin, then roll the pastry out into a circle about 35.5cm wide. Trim 1cm off the uneven pastry edge to neaten, then use the rolling pin to lift the dough on to a large piece of baking parchment. Use a 20.5cm cake tin or plate to gently press an indent into the centre of the pastry to mark out a circle. Evenly sprinkle semolina inside the circle and pile the rhubarb on top. Brush the 5cm pastry border with egg. Fold the border up and over the edge of the fruit, pinching a seam at 5cm intervals. Chill for 15min.

4. Brush the pastry rim with the remaining egg and sprinkle with demerara sugar. Carefully slide on to the preheated baking sheet and bake for 30–40min until golden.

5. Before serving, simmer the reserved rhubarb juice and 3tbsp water in a small pan for 3–4min until reduced to 1tbsp. Brush over the baked fruit to glaze. Serve warm, with custard.

Coconut and Blackberry Cheesecake

Using ricotta and yogurt creates a delicious, healthier version of traditional cheesecake.

15g unsalted butter, melted, plus extra to grease
75g bran flakes, crushed
125g caster sugar
1kg ricotta
200g Greek-style coconut yogurt
1 tbsp cornflour, sifted
3 large eggs, beaten
400g blackberries
Icing sugar, to dust

**Hands-on time: 15min, plus cooling and chilling
Cooking time: about 1hr 15min
Serves 10**

PER SERVING 301cals, 13g protein, 16g fat (9g saturates), 25g carbs (20g total sugars), 3g fibre

◆ GET AHEAD
Make to end of step 2 up to a day ahead. Complete recipe to serve.

1. Grease and line the sides of a 20.5cm springform cake tin with baking parchment. In a bowl, mix together the melted butter, bran flakes and 15g of the caster sugar. Empty into the prepared tin and spread evenly. Set aside.

2. Heat the oven to 150°C (130°C fan) mark 2. Put the remaining caster sugar, ricotta, yogurt, cornflour and eggs into a large bowl. Whisk together until smooth and combined. Carefully fold in 175g of the blackberries, then empty the mixture into the tin and level the surface. Bake for 1¼hr or until just set. Cool in the tin, then cover and chill for at least 2hr or overnight. Don't worry about any cracks – they'll be covered later.

3. Remove the cake from the tin and put on a serving plate. Peel off the parchment and top the cheesecake with the remaining berries. Dust with icing sugar, slice and serve.

Individual Apple Tarts

So tasty and impressive that your guests will never know you took a few shortcuts! These taste great with a scoop of vanilla ice cream or some pouring cream.

320g sheet all-butter puff pastry
125g Carnation Caramel
3 eating apples (we used Braeburns), quartered, cored and finely sliced
Icing sugar, to dust (optional)

Hands-on time: 15min
Cooking time: about 25min
Serves 6

PER TART 225cals, 4g protein, 10g fat (7g saturates), 30g carbs (18g total sugars), 1g fibre

1. Heat the oven to 200°C (180°C fan) mark 6. Line a baking sheet with baking parchment. Unroll the pastry and use a cutter to stamp out 6 x 11.5cm rounds (or use a similar-sized cup or bowl as a template). Transfer to the prepared baking sheet, spacing apart.

2. Lightly score a circle 1cm in from the edge of the pastry with a sharp knife or second smaller cutter (don't cut all the way through). Divide the caramel among the tarts and spread almost to the scored border. Neatly pile on the apple slices.

3. Bake for 25min until the pastry is golden and risen and the apples are tender. Lightly dust with icing sugar, if you like, and serve.

Cherry Bakewell Tart

Semolina mimics the texture of ground almonds here,
so even those avoiding nuts can enjoy this retro treat.

FOR THE PASTRY
200g plain flour, plus extra to dust
2 tbsp icing sugar, sifted
60g unsalted butter, chilled and cubed

FOR THE CHERRY COMPOTE
300g frozen cherries
2 tbsp caster sugar
Finely grated zest and juice ½ lemon, keep separate

FOR THE 'FRANGIPANE'
150g unsalted butter, softened
225g caster sugar
2 medium egg yolks
2 tsp vanilla bean paste
1 tbsp milk
150g dry semolina
2 tbsp plain flour
Finely grated zest 1 orange

FOR THE TOPPING
50g icing sugar
Pink food colouring paste/gel (optional)

Hands-on time: 45min, plus chilling and cooling
Cooking time: about 1hr 30min
Serves 8

PER SERVING 558cals, 6g protein, 23g fat (14g
saturates), 82g carbs (50g total sugars), 2g fibre

1. To make the pastry, pulse the flour, icing sugar
   and a pinch of salt in a food processor to combine.
   Add the butter and pulse until the mixture
   resembles fine breadcrumbs. Add 2½ tbsp cold
   water and pulse until the pastry begins to clump
   together. Empty on to a work surface, shape into
   a disc, wrap in clingfilm and chill for 30min.

2. For the cherry compote, heat the cherries,
   sugar and lemon juice in a pan over a low heat,
   stirring until the sugar dissolves. Turn up the
   heat to medium-high and bubble for 10min,
   until the cherries have started to break down
   and the liquid is syrupy. Remove from the heat,
   stir through the lemon zest and cool.

3. Lightly dust a work surface with flour and roll
   out the pastry, then use to line a 20.5cm round,
   4cm deep, loose-bottomed fluted tart tin. Leave
   any excess pastry hanging over the edges. Prick
   the base with a fork and chill for 10min.

4. Heat the oven to 200°C (180°C fan) mark 6. Line
   the pastry case with a large piece of baking
   parchment and fill with baking beans, then bake
   for 15–20min until sides are set. Carefully lift
   out the parchment and beans and return the
   tin to the oven for 5min until the pastry feels
   sandy to the touch and is lightly golden. Trim
   the excess pastry with a serrated knife, then
   set the tin aside to cool. Reduce the oven
   temperature to 180°C (160°C fan) mark 4.

5. To make the 'frangipane', beat the butter and
   sugar using a handheld electric whisk until pale
   and fluffy. Gradually beat in the yolks, then the

vanilla. Fold through the milk, semolina, flour and orange zest (the mixture will be thick).

6. Spread the compote into the base of the pastry case (still in its tin). Dollop over the 'frangipane' and level with your hands. Bake for 50min, until set. Cool in then tin for 20min, then transfer to a wire rack to cool completely.

7. For the topping, mix the icing sugar with enough water to form a thick icing that can still be drizzled. If you like, remove half to a separate bowl and dye it with pink food colouring. Drizzle or pipe the icing(s) over the top of the tart. Leave to set a little before serving.

Nectarine and Apricot Tart

This tart is so stunning that you won't miss the conventional creamy filling.

(V)

FOR THE PASTRY
150g plain flour, plus extra to dust
75g cold unsalted butter, cubed
1 tbsp caster sugar
1 egg yolk

FOR THE FILLING
175–200g apricot compote
3 ripe nectarines, halved and stones removed
Half-fat crème fraîche, to serve

Hands-on time: 25min, plus chilling and cooling
Cooking time: about 20min
Serves 6

PER SERVING 270cals, 4g protein, 12g fat (7g saturates), 36g carbs (16g total sugars), 3g fibre

◆ GET AHEAD
Make to end of step 2 up to a day ahead. Complete the recipe to serve.

1. Use a food processor to combine the flour and butter until the mixture resembles fine breadcrumbs. Empty into a bowl and stir in the sugar.

2. Using a blunt-ended knife, quickly stir in the yolk and 1–2 tbsp cold water. Tip on to a work surface and quickly bring together with your hands. Wrap in clingfilm and chill for 30min.

3. Heat the oven to 200°C (180°C fan) mark 6. Lightly flour a work surface and roll out the pastry to the thickness of a £1 coin. Use to line a 20.5cm diameter, 2.5cm deep loose-bottomed fluted tart tin – the pastry should hang over the edge of the tin. Prick the base with a fork. Line pastry with baking parchment and fill with baking beans. Bake for 10–12min until set, then remove the beans and parchment. Return the pastry to the oven and cook for 10min until golden. Cool on a wire rack.

4. Blend the apricot compote until smooth. Trim the pastry, lift out of the tin and put on a serving plate. Spoon in all but 1 tbsp of the compote and level the surface. Thinly slice the nectarine halves and arrange in circles on top of the compote. Brush the fruit with the remaining compote, then serve the tart in slices with half-fat crème fraîche.

Blueberry Custard Tart

This tart has Scandinavian influences, with rye pastry and soured cream in the custard. Freeze leftover egg whites in suitable bags ready to defrost for meringues or soufflés.

FOR THE PASTRY
100g plain flour, plus extra to dust
125g wholemeal rye flour
175g unsalted butter, cubed and chilled
50g caster sugar
1 large egg, separated

FOR THE FILLING
600ml double cream
300ml soured cream
9 large egg yolks
100g caster sugar
1 tsp vanilla extract
125g blueberries
Icing sugar, to dust (optional)

Hands-on time: 30min, plus chilling and cooling
Cooking time: about 1hr 30min
Serves 12

PER SERVING 587cals, 7g protein, 49g fat (29g saturates), 29g carbs (16g total sugars), 3g fibre

◆ GET AHEAD
Make the tart up to a day ahead. When cool, transfer to a serving plate and chill. Allow to come to room temperature before serving.

1. For the pastry, mix the flours together in a large bowl. Rub in the butter with your fingertips until it resembles breadcrumbs. Mix in the sugar, then the egg yolk and 1½ tbsp cold water until the pastry comes together. Knead briefly. Alternatively, pulse the butter and flours in a food processor until the mixture resembles breadcrumbs. Pulse in the sugar. Mix the yolk and 1½ tbsp cold water, then add to processor and pulse until the pastry clumps together. Remove from the processor bowl and knead briefly.

2. On a floured surface, roll out the pastry to line a 23cm round, 4cm deep fluted tart tin (wrap and reserve any spare pastry at room temperature). Chill the lined tin for 30min.

3. Heat the oven to 190°C (170°C fan) mark 5. Line the pastry with baking parchment and fill with baking beans. Put on a baking sheet, then bake blind for 18–20min until the pastry sides are set. Carefully remove the parchment and beans. Patch up any areas with reserved pastry if needed, then brush the pastry with some egg white and return to the oven for 2min until firm and glossy.

4. Lower the oven temperature to 140°C (120° fan) mark 1. In a small pan, mix the creams and bring to the boil. Meanwhile, mix the egg yolks and sugar in a medium heatproof bowl. Gradually pour over the hot cream mixture, whisking all the time. Strain through a sieve into a jug and stir in the vanilla.

5. Carefully pour the custard into the pastry case (still in its tin) and lightly scatter over the blueberries (so they float on the mixture). Bake in the oven for 65–70min until the custard is just set but has a slight wobble if the tin is tapped. Cool in the tin on a wire rack.

6. Remove the tart from the tin and transfer to a serving plate. Dust lightly with icing sugar, if you like, and serve at room temperature.

Proper Apple Pie

Just like mum used to make! This double-crusted pie tastes as homely and comforting as it looks.

FOR THE PASTRY
300g plain flour, plus extra to dust
200g unsalted butter, chilled and cut into cubes

FOR THE FILLING
1.4kg Bramley apples, peeled and cut into 2cm pieces
100g caster sugar, plus extra to sprinkle
1 tsp ground cinnamon
75g sultanas
1 medium egg, beaten
Double cream, to serve

**Hands-on time: 30min, plus chilling and cooling
Cooking time: about 50min
Serves 8**

PER SERVING 462cals, 5g protein 22g fat (13g saturates), 59g carbs (30g total sugars), 4g fibre

◆ GH TIP
If you prefer a lattice top, cut the rolled-out lid pastry into 2.5cm thick strips and weave a criss-cross pattern over the apple filling to create a basket effect.

1. Put the flour, 175g of the butter and a pinch of salt into a food processor and pulse until the mixture resembles fine breadcrumbs. Alternatively, rub the butter into the flour using your fingers. Add 3–4 tbsp ice-cold water and whizz again (or mix with a blunt-ended cutlery knife) until the pastry just comes together. Tip on to a work surface, bring together and wrap in clingfilm. Chill for 30min.

2. Meanwhile, put the apple pieces into a large frying pan with the remaining 25g butter, the sugar and the cinnamon. Cook gently for about 10min until the apples are just tender and there's barely any moisture in the pan. Add the sultanas and leave to cool completely.

3. Heat the oven to 200°C (180°C fan) mark 6 and put a baking sheet on the middle shelf to heat up. Lightly dust a work surface with flour and roll out two-thirds of the pastry. Use it to line a 20.5cm round, 7cm deep springform cake tin. Spoon the cooled apple mixture into the tin, level the surface, then fold the excess pastry over the apples. Roll out the remaining pastry as before, until it's larger than the base of the tin, then put the tin on the pastry and cut around the base. Lay the pastry circle on top of the apple mixture and press the edges down. If you like, cut apple and letter shapes from the pastry trimmings and stick on to pie.

4. Cut a small cross in the middle of the lid to allow steam to escape. Brush the top of the pie with beaten egg and sprinkle over some sugar. Put the tin into the oven on the heated baking sheet. Bake for 35–40min until golden.

5. Leave the pie to cool for 10min in the tin, then take it out of the tin and serve it warm or at room temperature with lashings of cream, if you like.

Strawberry Tart

No tea party would be complete without a scrumptious strawberry tart as the centrepiece.

175g plain flour, plus extra to dust
125g unsalted butter, chilled and cubed
40g caster sugar
1 medium egg, separated

FOR THE CRÈME PÂTISSIÈRE
60g caster sugar
2 medium egg yolks
25g cornflour
250ml semi-skimmed milk
1 vanilla pod, halved lengthways
150ml double cream

FOR THE TOPPING
About 400g strawberries (ideally the same size), hulled
75g strawberry jam, sieved

Hands-on time: 45min, plus chilling and cooling
Cooking time: about 40min
Serves 10

PER SERVING 338cals, 4g protein, 21g fat (13g saturates), 35g carbs (20g total sugars), 1g fibre

◆ GET AHEAD
Bake the pastry case up to a day ahead. Cool, then loosely wrap tin in clingfilm and store at room temperature. Assemble up to 2hr ahead and chill, leaving the glaze until just before serving.

1. Whizz the flour and butter in a processor until the mixture resembles fine breadcrumbs. Alternatively, rub the butter into the flour using your fingers. Add the sugar and whizz or stir to combine. Add the egg yolk and 3 tsp cold water and pulse or stir with a blunt-ended cutlery knife until the pastry comes together. Shape into a disc, wrap in clingfilm and chill for 30min.

2. Meanwhile, make the crème pâtissière. Mix the sugar, yolks and cornflour in a medium heatproof bowl until smooth. Heat the milk and vanilla pod until just boiling, whisking occasionally to encourage the seeds out of the pod. Gradually add the milk to the egg mixture, whisking constantly. Return to the pan and, whisking non-stop, bubble until thickened. Scrape into a large heatproof bowl, remove the pod, cool and chill.

3. Roll out the pastry on a lightly floured surface and use to line a 23cm round springform tin. Trim the pastry to come about 3cm up the sides. Prick the base all over with a fork, then chill for 15min.

4. Heat the oven to 190°C (170°C fan) mark 5. Line the pastry base with greaseproof paper and fill with baking beans. Bake for 20min, then remove the paper and beans and return to the oven for 10min. Remove from the oven and brush the inside of the pastry with egg white, then return to the oven for 3min. Cool in the tin, then transfer the pastry case to a serving plate or cake stand.

5. To assemble, whizz the crème pâtissière until smooth, then return to the large bowl, or beat in the bowl with a handheld electric whisk. Whip the double cream in a separate bowl until stiff, then fold into the crème pâtissière. Spoon into the pastry case, level the surface, and chill for 30min until set.

6. To serve, arrange the strawberries on top of the tart and glaze with the jam.

10

Christmas Baking

Minty White Chocolate Meringue Roulade

It's hard to resist such pillowy perfection! If you're not a fan of peppermint, just leave it out.

FOR THE ROULADE
4 large egg whites
175g caster sugar
1½ tsp gluten-free cornflour
1 tsp white wine vinegar
4 tbsp icing sugar
200ml double cream
Peppermint extract, to taste
100g white chocolate, grated

TO DECORATE (optional)
Few mint leaves or small mint sprigs
1 large egg white
Caster sugar, to sprinkle

Hands-on time: 30min, plus overnight drying and cooling
Cooking time: 15min
Serves 6

PER SERVING 424cals, 4g protein, 23g fat (14g saturates), 50g carbs (49g total sugars), no fibre

◆ GET AHEAD
Prepare to the end of step 6 up to a day ahead. Loosely cover with foil and chill. Complete the recipe to serve (re-dusting with icing sugar if needed).

1. If making the decoration, lightly brush mint leaves/sprigs on both sides with egg white (don't dip) then sprinkle well with caster sugar to coat evenly. Leave to harden overnight on a baking sheet lined with baking parchment.

2. To make the roulade, heat the oven to 180°C (160°C fan) mark 4 and line a 23 x 33cm Swiss roll tin with baking parchment.

3. In a large, grease-free bowl, beat the egg whites to stiff peaks using a handheld electric whisk. Gradually add the caster sugar, whisking to stiff peaks after each addition – the meringue should be thick and glossy. Quickly whisk in the gluten-free cornflour and vinegar. Spread into the prepared tin, smoothing to level.

4. Bake for 15min until puffed and firm. Cool for 10min in the tin (the meringue will sink on cooling), then lift the meringue (in its parchment) on to a wire rack to cool completely.

5. Lay a sheet of baking parchment larger than the meringue on a work surface. Dust evenly with half the icing sugar. Invert the meringue on to the paper, then peel away the lining paper.

6. In a medium bowl, whip the cream, the remaining icing sugar and peppermint extract (a little goes a long way!) to soft peaks. Spread over the meringue and sprinkle over most of the chocolate. With the help of the paper, roll up the roulade from one of the short edges. Transfer to a serving plate.

7. Sprinkle over the remaining chocolate and decorate with mint leaves, if using.

Stollen Crinkle Biscuits

Nothing evokes Christmas like the flavours of stollen, and we've put them into these eye-catching biscuits. Swap the brandy for apple juice, if you prefer.

V

50g mixed dried fruit
15g chopped mixed peel
15g dried sour cherries, roughly chopped
3 tbsp brandy
75g unsalted butter
175g caster sugar
2 medium eggs
250g plain flour
1 tsp baking powder
25g icing sugar, plus extra to dust
100g golden marzipan

Hands-on time: 15min, plus soaking, chilling and cooling
Cooking time: about 30min
Makes 20

PER BISCUIT 158cals, 2g protein, 4g fat (2g saturates), 26g carbs (16g total sugars), 1g fibre

◆ TO STORE
Keep in an airtight container at room temperature for up to 5 days (they will soften on storing).

◆ TO GIFT
Pack into a lined tin or Cellophane bags.

1. In a medium bowl, mix the dried fruit, mixed peel, cherries and brandy. Set aside to soak for 1hr.

2. Melt the butter in a small pan, then pour into a medium bowl and set aside to cool for 5min. Stir in the caster sugar, followed by the eggs, one at a time.

3. Drain the soaked fruit and mix into the sugar mixture. Stir in the flour, baking powder and a pinch of salt. Cover and chill for 1hr.

4. Heat the oven to 180°C (160°C fan) mark 4 and line 3 baking sheets with baking parchment. Put the icing sugar into a small bowl. Divide both the marzipan and biscuit dough into 20 evenly sized pieces. If the dough is sticky, dust your hands with a little icing sugar as you work.

5. In the palm of your hand, flatten a portion of biscuit dough and put a piece of marzipan in the centre. Draw up the edges of the dough to enclose the marzipan, then roll into a ball. Repeat with the remaining dough and marzipan. Roll the balls in the icing sugar, then arrange, spaced apart, on the lined baking sheets. Dust any remaining icing sugar over the biscuits.

6. Bake for 20-25min, until lightly golden. Allow to cool on sheets for 5min before transferring to a wire rack to cool completely.

Pistachio and Cranberry Stollen Wreath

An irresistible centrepiece traditionally served with butter at breakfast. We've used pistachios to make our marzipan for a colourful and delicious alternative – great for those who fancy something a little bit different!

FOR THE DOUGH
300g strong white bread flour, plus extra to dust
7g sachet fast-action dried yeast
2 tbsp mixed spice
Finely grated zest 1 lemon
Finely grated zest 1 orange
75g unsalted butter, melted, plus 25g to brush
150ml whole milk
100g dried cranberries
100g raisins

FOR THE PISTACHIO MARZIPAN
200g pistachios
200g icing sugar, plus extra to dust
1 large egg

Hands-on time: 35min, plus rising and cooling
Cooking time: about 25min
Serves 8

PER SERVING 563cals, 12g protein, 24g fat (8g saturates), 74g carbs (44g total sugars), 4g fibre

◆ TO STORE
Keep well-wrapped in foil at room temperature for up to 2 days.

◆ GET AHEAD
Make, knead and cover the dough up to 24hr ahead. Chill. Allow to come to room temperature before completing.

1. To make the dough, mix the flour, yeast, mixed spice, zests and 1tsp fine salt in a large bowl. Add the melted butter and milk and mix to form a dough. Tip on to a lightly floured surface and knead for 5–10min, until smooth and elastic. Return to the bowl, cover with clingfilm and leave to rise in a warm place until doubled in size, about 1½hr.

2. Meanwhile, make the marzipan. Whizz the pistachios and icing sugar in a food processor until finely ground. Add the egg and pulse to make a thick paste. Cover and set aside.

3. Line a large baking sheet with baking parchment. Clear a large area of work surface and dust lightly with flour. Scrape out the dough, knead briefly, then roll out to a long thin rectangle, about 60 x 20.5cm. Dot marzipan evenly over the surface and, with slightly damp hands, spread it out as evenly as you can, leaving a 2.5cm border along the long edges. Sprinkle over the dried fruit, pressing it down a little.

4. Roll the dough up tightly from one of the long edges, working in sections if you need to. Position seam-side down. Leaving one end attached, slice in half lengthways, then arrange the strips so they are cut-side up. Holding a strip in each hand (and keeping them cut-side up), twist the strips, lifting the right-hand strip over the left, simultaneously moving the left strip to the right. Repeat this process until the strips

are fully twisted. Bring the 2 ends together to form a circle and pinch firmly to join. Carefully transfer to lined sheet, reshaping as needed. Cover with a clean, damp tea towel and leave to rise for 1–1¼hr until puffed. Heat the oven to 180°C (160°C fan) mark 4.

5. Uncover the stollen and bake for 25min, until golden. Remove from the oven and brush with melted butter. Cover with a clean, dry tea towel (this helps keep the stollen soft) and leave to cool. Dust with icing sugar to serve.

Classic Mince Pies

We've used a star cutter to stamp out the pastry
tops for these traditional mince pies, but you could
also use holly or Christmas tree shapes, if you like.

175g plain flour, plus extra to dust
75g cold butter, cubed
25g icing sugar, plus extra to dust
Finely grated zest of 1 orange
2 medium eggs
About 150g mincemeat
Icing sugar, to dust

Hands-on time: 30min, plus cooling
Cooking time: 20min
Makes 8 pies

PER PIE 232cals, 4g protein, 10g fat (5g saturates),
31g carbs (14g total sugars), 1g fibre

1. To make the pastry, put the flour, butter, icing
   sugar and orange zest into a food processor
   and whizz until the mixture resembles fine
   breadcrumbs. Add one egg and pulse until the
   pastry starts to clump together. Tip on to a work
   surface and bring together with your hands.

2. Heat the oven to 200°C (180°C fan) mark 6. Roll
   out the pastry thinly on a lightly floured surface
   and cut out 8 rounds using a 7.5cm fluted cutter.
   Use these to line 8 holes of a 12-hole bun tin.
   Divide the mincemeat among the cases.

3. Re-roll the pastry trimmings and cut out 8 stars
   using a 4.5–5cm star cutter. Put a star on top
   of the mincemeat. Lightly beat the remaining
   egg and brush some of it over the tops of the
   pastry stars.

4. Bake for 15–20min or until golden and crisp.
   Allow pies to cool slightly before removing from
   the tin and dust with icing sugar before serving
   warm or at room temperature.

Christmas Bauble Hanging Biscuits

Whether making decorations for your tree, packaging biscuits as a beautiful gift or simply enjoying an extra seasonal treat, this is a sugar cookie recipe you can trust.

75g butter, softened, plus extra to grease
100g caster sugar
40g golden syrup
1 medium egg
1 tsp vanilla bean paste
Finely grated zest and juice 1 lemon (keep separate)
225g plain flour, plus extra to dust
½ tsp baking powder

TO DECORATE
500g royal icing sugar
Red food colouring paste
Silver dragees

Hands-on time: 1hr, plus chilling, cooling and setting
Cooking time: about 15min
Makes about 24 biscuits

PER BISCUIT 166cals, 1g protein, 3g fat (2g saturates), 34g carbs (26g total sugars), no fibre

◆ TO STORE
Once the icing has set, store in an airtight container at room temperature for up to 2 weeks. The biscuits will soften faster if they are exposed to the air.

◆ GH TIP
To harden the flood icing faster, return the biscuits, icing-side up, to a baking sheet. Put in an oven heated to its lowest setting, about 110°C (90°C fan) mark ¼, for 30min or until the icing is set hard.

1. In a large bowl, beat the butter, sugar and golden syrup using a handheld electric whisk until pale and fluffy. Next, beat in the egg, vanilla and zest. Sift over the flour and baking powder and mix until just combined, then tip on to a clean work surface and bring together with your hands. Wrap in clingfilm and chill for at least 30min or up to 24hr.

2. Line 2 large baking sheets with baking parchment. Lightly flour a work surface and roll out the dough until 5mm thick. Stamp out Christmas shapes, re-rolling trimmings as needed. Arrange the biscuits on prepared sheets, spacing a little apart. If you are planning on hanging the biscuits, make a 5mm hole in the top of each with a skewer. Chill for 30min, until firm.

3. Heat the oven to 180°C (160°C fan) mark 4. Bake the biscuits for 15min until lightly golden. Transfer to a wire rack to cool completely.

4. For the icing, sift the icing sugar into a large bowl. Using a handheld electric whisk on the lowest speed, beat in 5-6 tbsp of the lemon juice (mixed with cold water, if there's not enough) to make a thick, smooth icing. Beat for a further 3-4min until shiny; it should have the consistency of toothpaste. Spoon a third of the icing into a separate bowl; this is your outline icing. If you like, divide the outline mixture in half again and dye one batch red with food colouring. Transfer the outline icings to separate piping bags fitted with fine nozzles. Whisk a little more water (2-3 tbsp) into the remaining

two-thirds of the icing, until you have a thick but pourable consistency. This is your flood icing. Again, dye half of this red in a separate bowl, if you like. Transfer to 2 separate piping bags.

5. To flood-decorate sections, or the whole biscuit, pipe an unbroken line using the outline icing (including making a circle around any ribbon hole). Snip off the end of a flood icing bag and fill the space within the outline. Use a toothpick

to nudge the icing into any gaps (store the piping bags in bowls with the cut ends facing up while you're working). Allow to set before decorating further with outline icing and silver dragees. Repeat with the remaining biscuits. Leave to set firm. (see GH TIP)

6. If you've made holes, thread through ribbon and hang.

Zimtsterne

These chewy, gluten-free stars are a staple of German
Christmas markets. Use ready-ground hazelnuts,
if you can find them.

100g blanched hazelnuts
2 medium egg whites
200g icing sugar, sifted, plus extra to dust
150g ground almonds
2 tsp ground cinnamon
1 tsp ground ginger
Finely grated zest ½ lemon

Hands-on time: 40min, plus cooling and setting
Cooking time: about 10min
Makes about 45 stars

PER BISCUIT 55cals, 1g protein, 3g fat (no saturates),
5g carbs (5g total sugars), 0.4g fibre

◆ TO STORE
Keep in an airtight container at room temperature
for up to 2 weeks.

1. Heat the oven to 130°C conventional heat
   (do not use a fan setting, as this will cause
   the glaze to brown too quickly) mark ½. Line
   2 large baking sheets with baking parchment.
   Whizz the hazelnuts in a food processor until
   finely ground (don't overwork them or they
   will become greasy). Set aside.

2. In a large bowl with a handheld electric whisk,
   beat the egg whites until they hold soft peaks.
   Add the sugar, beating on a low speed until
   incorporated, then beat on full power for 2min.
   Spoon out 50g of mixture to use as a glaze.

3. Using a large spoon, mix the nuts, spices and
   zest into remaining mixture to make a stiff,
   slightly sticky dough. Lightly dust a sheet of
   baking parchment with icing sugar and set the
   dough on top. Lightly dust the dough with icing
   sugar and cover with another sheet of baking
   parchment (this makes rolling out easier).

4. Roll out until 5mm thick. Remove the top paper
   and stamp out stars using a 4cm cutter. Dip
   the cutter in icing sugar if it's sticking.

5. Transfer stars to the prepared sheets (they don't
   spread much). Paint the top of each star with the
   reserved glaze in an even, thin layer.

6. Bake for 10min in the lower half of the oven or
   until the biscuits feel firmer and the glaze is set
   but not browning. Cool on trays before serving.

Coconut Snowball Cake

This novel method creates a light, fluffy sponge, while
the Swiss meringue buttercream is silky smooth.

(V)

FOR THE CAKE
175g unsalted butter, chopped and at room temperature,
   plus extra to grease
350g plain flour
225g granulated sugar
2 tsp baking powder
6 medium egg whites
300ml full-fat coconut milk
60g desiccated coconut
1 tsp vanilla extract

FOR THE FILLING
150g lemon curd

FOR THE FROSTING AND TO DECORATE
3 medium egg whites
125g granulated sugar
150g unsalted butter, at room temperature, cut
   into 2cm pieces
1 tsp vanilla extract
60ml full-fat coconut milk
50g desiccated coconut
Ferrero Raffaellos (optional)

Hands-on time: 1hr, plus cooling
Cooking time: about 45min
Cuts into 16 slices

PER SLICE 435cals, 5g protein, 26g fat (18g saturates),
45g carbs (28g total sugars), 2g fibre

◆ TO STORE
Keep the iced cake, loosely covered, in the fridge
for up 3 days. Serve at room temperature.

◆ GET AHEAD
Make the cakes and frosting up to a day ahead.
Wrap the cool cakes in clingfilm and store in a tin
at room temperature. Cover and chill the frosting;
bring to room temperature and beat before
completing the recipe.

1. Heat the oven to 180°C (160°C fan) mark 4.
   Grease and line 2 x 20.5cm round cake tins
   with baking parchment.

2. In a freestanding mixer fitted with a whisk, mix
   the flour, sugar, baking powder and ¼ tsp fine salt
   on low to combine (or use a large bowl and a
   handheld electric whisk). Add the butter and mix
   until the mixture resembles large breadcrumbs.

3. In a large jug, whisk the egg whites, coconut milk,
   desiccated coconut and vanilla until combined.

4. Add half the coconut mixture to the dry
   ingredients and beat on medium-high for
   20sec until combined. Scrape down the sides
   of the bowl. Add the remaining coconut mixture
   and beat on medium-high for 1min, until light
   and fluffy.

5. Divide the batter evenly between the tins and
   bake for 35min or until a skewer inserted into
   the centre comes out clean. Cool in tins on
   a wire rack.

6. For the frosting, in a large heatproof bowl set
   over a pan of barely simmering water, beat the
   egg whites and sugar with a handheld electric
   whisk until mixture is warm and sugar has
   dissolved, about 5min.

7. Quickly empty into a freestanding mixer, or continue with the bowl off the heat and a handheld electric mixer. Beat on high for 10min or until the meringue is thick and the outside of the bowl is completely cool. Gradually add the butter, one piece at a time, beating well after each addition. (If the frosting looks curdled, carry on beating – it will come together.) Once all butter is in, beat on medium-high for 4min. Add the vanilla and coconut milk and beat for 2min until thick and smooth.

8. Slice the cakes in half horizontally and sandwich back together with lemon curd. Spread the frosting over the top and sides of the cake, then press desiccated coconut on to the sides. Decorate with Raffaellos, if using, and serve.

No-soak Christmas Cake

This recipe uses a microwave to speed up preparation time. If you don't have one, cover the fruit bowl with clingfilm and leave it to soak in a warm place overnight.

150g butter, softened, plus extra to grease
350g each sultanas and raisins
100g each prunes, dried apricots and dates,
    finely chopped
150ml brandy, plus extra to drizzle
Finely grated zest and juice 1 lemon
175g dark brown soft sugar
3 medium eggs, beaten
125g self-raising flour
1½ tbsp black treacle
1 tsp mixed spice
1 tsp ground cinnamon

Hands-on time: 30min
Cooking time: about 3hr 30min
Cuts into 20 slices

PER SLICE 272cals, 3g protein, 7g fat (4.5g saturates), 44g carbs (39g total sugars), 2g fibre

◆ GH TIP
The cake will keep for up to 3 months stored as described in step 6. It can be doused in alcohol every week if you prefer a stronger taste.

1. Heat the oven to 150°C (130°C fan) mark 2. Grease and double-line a 20.5cm cake tin with baking parchment, making sure the parchment comes 5cm above the top of the tin. Wrap a double layer of parchment around the outside of the tin and secure it with string – this will help stop the cake from burning.

2. Put all the fruit into a large microwave-safe bowl, then stir in the brandy, lemon zest and juice. Microwave on full power, stirring halfway through, for 2½ minutes or until the fruit has absorbed the liquid.

3. In a large bowl, beat the butter and sugar together using a handheld electric mixer or wooden spoon until light and fluffy, about 5min. Gradually beat in the eggs – if the mixture looks as if it might curdle, whisk in a little of the flour. Then beat in the black treacle.

4. Sift the flour and spices into the butter mixture and fold in using a large metal spoon, then fold in the soaked fruit. Spoon the cake mixture into the prepared tin and level the surface. Use the handle of a wooden spoon to make a rough hole in the centre of the mix to help keep the top of the cake level during baking.

5. Bake for 3–3½hr or until a skewer inserted into the centre comes out clean. Cover the cake with foil if it is browning too quickly. Leave to cool in the tin for 10 minutes, then take out and allow to cool completely on a wire rack, leaving the baking parchment wrapped round the outside of the cake.

6. To store, wrap a few layers of clingfilm around the cooled cake (still in its parchment), then cover with foil. Store in an airtight container in a cool place. After 2 weeks, unwrap the cake. Prick all over with a skewer and pour over 1 tbsp brandy. Rewrap and store as before (see GH TIP).

Red Velvet Snowflakes

A version of the ever-popular cake that is reminiscent of Bourbon biscuits. Need we say more?

FOR THE BISCUITS
75g unsalted butter, softened
100g caster sugar
1 medium egg
40g buttermilk
¾ tsp red food colouring paste
175g plain flour, plus extra to dust
1 tsp baking powder
25g cocoa

FOR THE ICING
200g icing sugar, sifted

**Hands-on time: 45min, plus overnight chilling, cooling
  and setting.**
Cooking time: about 12min
Makes about 18 biscuits

PER BISCUIT 118cals, 2g protein, 4g fat (3g saturates),
18g carbs (11g total sugars), 1g fibre

◆ TO STORE
Keep in an airtight container at room temperature
for up to 2 weeks.

1. In a large bowl, beat the butter and caster sugar with a handheld electric whisk until pale and fluffy. Add the egg, buttermilk and food colouring and beat to combine. Fold in the remaining biscuit ingredients, then bring together with your hands. Wrap the dough in clingfilm and chill overnight.

2. Heat the oven to 180°C (160°C fan) mark 4. Line 2 large baking sheets with baking parchment. Unwrap the dough and lightly dust with flour. Roll out between 2 large pieces of baking parchment until 3mm thick. Stamp out 9cm snowflake shapes, brushing off any excess flour. Use a palette knife to transfer to the prepared sheets, spacing about 4cm apart – you may need to bake the biscuits in batches.

3. Bake for 10–12 minutes until sandy to the touch. Cool for 5min on the sheets before transferring to a wire rack to cool completely.

4. To ice, mix the icing sugar with 2tbsp hot water to make a thick icing. Scrape into a piping bag with a small plain nozzle (or just snip off the end of a disposable piping bag). Pipe patterns on to the biscuits and leave to set.

Magical Forest Christmas Cake

Turn your fruitcake into a stunning winter scene with these
fun-to-make trees. The key is to use royal icing, which sets firmer
than regular icing sugar and is easier to pipe.

20.5cm fruit cake (see the No-soak Christmas Cake
   on previous page)
2-3 tbsp apricot glaze
750g pack royal icing sugar
500g natural or golden marzipan

FOR THE DECORATIONS
About 300g royal icing sugar
Paste/gel food colouring in forest shades – we used teal,
   spruce green and holly green
White lollipop sticks
Silver dragees and/or sugar snowflake sprinkles

TO FINISH (optional)
Silver taper candles
Edible silver glitter spray – we used Cake Décor

Hands-on time: 1hr, plus overnight drying
Serves 20

◆ GET AHEAD
Assemble up to 2 weeks ahead.

1. Put the cake on a stand or board and spread
the top and sides with apricot glaze. Sift a little
of the royal icing sugar on to a work surface
and roll out the marzipan until it's large enough
to cover the cake. Lay over the cake and smooth
with your hands to ease out creases, then trim
the excess. Allow to air dry for at least 2hr, or
ideally overnight.

2. Next, make the tree decorations. Line 2 baking
sheets with baking parchment. In a large bowl,
beat 300g royal icing sugar and 4 tbsp cold
water with a handheld electric whisk until very
thick but just pipeable (adjust as needed with
more royal icing sugar or water). Divide among
small bowls (use one for each colour) and dye
each a different shade of green.

3. Place a lollipop stick on to a lined sheet.
Scrape the first icing into a piping bag fitted
with a fine plain or star nozzle. Starting at the
top and working over the stick, pipe downwards
in conjoined horizontal lines, increasing their
width as you go to make a triangular tree. While
still wet, decorate some trees with dragees or
sugar sprinkles. Repeat with the remaining icing
and different shades, varying the nozzles and
sizes of the trees, if you like. Allow to dry at
room temperature to set hard, about 24hr.

4. Once the trees have set hard, make up the
remaining 750g pack royal icing according to
the pack instructions. Spread over the marzipan-
covered cake, keeping the icing fairly peaky.

5. While the icing is wet, carefully peel the set
trees off the baking paper and press them into
the top of the cake, trimming the sticks first to
create trees of different heights. Push in candles,
if using, then let the icing set.

6. To finish, dust the trees and cake with glitter
spray, if you like.

Chocolate Shortbread Trees

Kids will love making and decorating these stacked
biscuit trees – and eating them, too!

FOR THE BISCUITS
250g unsalted butter, chilled and chopped
150g caster sugar
400g plain flour, plus extra to dust
4 tbsp cocoa powder

TO DECORATE
150g white chocolate
25g pistachios, roughly chopped

**Hands-on time: 45min, plus chilling, cooling
 and setting
Cooking time: about 20min
Makes 8 trees**

PER TREE (average) 639cals, 9g protein, 36g fat
(21g saturates), 69g carbs (30g total sugars), 3g fibre

◆ TO STORE
Keep in an airtight container at room temperature
for up to a week.

1. Whizz the biscuit ingredients in a food processor
   until the mixture starts to clump together. Tip
   on to a lightly floured work surface and knead
   to make a smooth dough. Wrap in clingfilm
   and chill for 1hr.

2. Heat the oven to 180°C (160°C fan) mark 4
   and line 2 large baking sheets with baking
   parchment. Roll out the dough on a lightly
   floured work surface until 7.5mm thick.
   Stamp out 16 x 7.5cm stars, 16 x 6.5cm stars
   and 16 x 4cm stars, re-rolling the trimmings
   as needed. Arrange on prepared sheets (they
   don't spread much); bake for 10–12min, or until
   sandy to the touch (they will firm on cooling).
   Leave to cool completely on sheets.

3. Melt the chocolate in a heatproof bowl set over
   a pan of barely simmering water. To assemble
   the trees, use the melted chocolate as glue and
   stick together 2 large stars, offsetting the points.
   Next stick on 2 medium stars in a similar
   fashion, followed by 2 small stars to make a star
   tree. Repeat with the remaining stars to make
   8 trees. Drizzle over remaining white chocolate
   and sprinkle over pistachios. Leave to set. If
   giving as a gift, wrap in Cellophane bags and
   tie with a ribbon.

Gingerbread Christmas Pudding

We've warmed up our pudding with gingerbread spices and included a luscious ginger caramel sauce if you want to add extra wow factor.

V

175g raisins
175g sultanas
100g Medjool dates, stoned and finely chopped
25g chopped mixed peel
100ml apple juice
50ml brandy
Butter, to grease
150g grated apple
2 tsp ground cinnamon
2 tsp mixed spice
2 tsp ground ginger
3 balls stem ginger, drained and finely chopped
100g dark brown soft sugar
75g treacle
75g golden syrup
100g plain flour
75g fresh white breadcrumbs
1 large egg, beaten
25g vegetarian suet

FOR THE GINGER CARAMEL SAUCE
50g caster sugar
150ml double cream
15g unsalted butter
3 tbsp ginger syrup (from a jar of stem ginger)

Hands-on time: 25min, plus overnight soaking, cooling and maturing
Cooking time: about 4hr 30min
Serves 8

PER SERVING (without sauce) 408cals, 5g protein, 4g fat (2g saturates), 83g carbs (68g total sugars), 3g fibre
PER SERVING (1 tbsp sauce) 74cals, 0g protein, 6g fat (4g saturates), 5g carbs (5g total sugars), 0g fibre

1. Put the dried fruit, mixed peel, apple juice and brandy into a large non-metallic bowl. Mix, cover and leave to soak overnight at room temperature.

2. Grease a 900ml pudding basin and line the base with a disc of baking parchment. Put a 30.5cm square of foil on top of a square of baking parchment the same size. Fold a 4cm pleat in the centre and set aside.

3. Add the remaining ingredients to the soaked fruit, mixing well. Transfer to the basin and press down. Put the foil and paper (foil-side up) on top and smooth down to cover. Tie a long piece of string securely under the lip of the basin and loop over the top to create a handle.

4. To cook, put a heatproof saucer into a large pan that has a tight-fitting lid. Lower in the pudding and pour in water to come halfway up the sides of the basin. Cover with the lid, bring to a boil and simmer for 4½hr, topping up the water as necessary.

5. Remove the pudding from the pan and leave to cool completely. Wrap the entire basin in a layer of clingfilm followed by a layer of foil. Store in a cool, dark place and leave to mature for up to 2 months.

6. To make the ginger caramel sauce, heat the sugar with 50ml water in a heavy-bottomed pan, stirring until the sugar dissolves. Turn up the heat and bubble until the mixture turns a deep caramel colour – swirl the pan rather than stirring at this stage. Remove from the heat and slowly stir in the double cream, followed by the butter and ginger syrup. Return to the heat, stirring to dissolve any hardened sugar, and bubble for a few minutes. Take off the

heat and cool slightly. Serve warm or at room temperature, poured over the pudding or alongside it. The cooled sauce will keep in the fridge for up to 1 day – reheat gently to serve.

◆ TO REHEAT THE PUDDING

Remove the clingfilm and foil and re-cover with a new lid as per the instructions in steps 2 and 3. Following method in step 4, steam for 1½hr until piping hot in the centre when pierced with a skewer. Remove from the pan and leave

to sit for 5min. Remove the lid and invert on to a serving plate. Peel off the baking parchment and serve with Ginger Caramel Sauce, if you like.

◆ TO FLAME YOUR PUDDING

Pour 50ml fresh brandy, rum or whisky into a large metal ladle. Warm carefully over a low gas hob. Alternatively, heat the alcohol in a small pan. Carefully light the alcohol using a gas lighter or long match and slowly pour over the pudding.

Crumble-topped Mince Pies

Orange zest adds a zingy freshness to the pastry.

175g plain flour, plus extra to dust
75g icing sugar
100g butter, chilled and cubed
1 medium egg yolk
Finely grated zest 1 orange, plus 1 tbsp juice
500g mincemeat

FOR THE CRUMBLE
75g plain flour
60g butter, cubed
4 tbsp demerara sugar
¼ tsp ground cinnamon
2 tbsp milk

Hands-on time: 25min, plus chilling and cooling
Cooking time: about 22min
Makes 24 pies

PER PIE 173cals, 1g protein, 7g fat (4g saturates),
26g carbs (18g total sugars), 1g fibre

◆ GET AHEAD
Store the cooled pies in an airtight container for
up to 5 days, or put in a freezerproof container,
separating with layers of baking parchment, and
freeze for up to 3 months. To serve, reheat from
frozen on a baking tray at 180°C (160°C) mark 4
for 10–12min until warmed through.

1. Pulse the flour, icing sugar and butter in a
   food processor until the mixture resembles fine
   breadcrumbs (or rub the butter into the flour and
   sugar using your fingers). Add the yolk, orange
   zest and juice, then pulse/mix until the pastry just
   comes together. Tip on to a work surface, shape
   into a disc, wrap in clingfilm and chill for 30min.

2. Meanwhile, make the crumble topping. In the
   small bowl of a food processor, pulse the flour,
   butter, sugar and cinnamon until they clump
   together (or rub the butter into the flour with
   your fingertips, then stir in sugar and
   cinnamon). Chill.

3. Heat the oven to 190°C (170°C fan) mark 5.
   Divide the pastry in half and, working with
   one piece at a time (keep the other chilled), roll
   out on a lightly floured surface until 3mm thick.
   Stamp out 24 fluted rounds using a 7.5cm cutter,
   re-rolling the trimmings as needed. Use the
   rounds to line 2 x 12-hole bun tins, then fill with
   mincemeat (a scant 1 tbsp per pie). Top each pie
   with crumble mixture and brush lightly with milk.

4. Bake for 20–22min until golden. Cool the pies
   in the tin for a few minutes, then carefully
   transfer to a wire rack to cool. Serve just warm
   or at room temperature.

Frosty Robin Cake

Remember to factor in drying times for the icing when beginning your cake decoration.

2–3 tbsp apricot jam
20.5cm fruit cake (see the No-soak Christmas Cake on p266)
Icing sugar, to dust
500g natural or golden marzipan
500g white sugarpaste icing
Brandy, gin, vodka or cooled boiled water, to brush

TO DECORATE
About 75g green sugarpaste icing
About 30g red sugarpaste icing
About 70g brown sugarpaste icing
About 20g white sugarpaste icing
Edible glue
About 5g orange or yellow sugarpaste icing
2–3 Flake chocolate bars

YOU'LL ALSO NEED
4½–6cm veined holly or ivy plunge cutter, or both (we also used a tiny ivy one)
Small paintbrush
Green and red lustre dust (optional)
Ribbon (optional)

Hands-on time: 1hr 30min, plus at least 2 days of overnight drying
Serves 20

◆ GH TIP
To check whether your rolled-out marzipan or sugarpaste will cover the cake, cut a piece of string long enough to go up one side of the cake, over the top centre and down the opposite side. Lay this string on the marzipan/sugarpaste and roll it out to this diameter.

1. A few days before you want to make the cake decoration, gently warm the jam in a small pan to loosen. Pass through a sieve into a small bowl. Put the cake on a board and brush the top and sides with sieved jam. Set aside.

2. Lightly dust a work surface with icing sugar and roll out the marzipan until it's large enough to cover the cake (see GH TIP). Lift on to the cake and gently smooth into position with your hands. Trim away any excess. Leave overnight at room temperature for the marzipan to harden slightly.

3. On the same day, line a baking sheet with baking parchment and lightly scrunch some foil into small sausages. Lightly dust a work surface with icing sugar and roll out the green sugarpaste until it is 3mm thick. Stamp out holly or ivy leaves (or both) and lay over the foil sausages on the lined baking sheet, to help give the leaves some movement (A). Reroll and stamp out trimmings (you need about 25 leaves). If you've made holly leaves, use about 5g of the red sugarpaste to make tiny balls for the holly berries and add to the lined sheet. Leave to harden overnight.

4. When your marzipan has hardened, lightly dust a work surface with icing sugar and roll out the 500g white sugarpaste until large enough to cover the cake. Brush the marzipan with brandy/gin/vodka/water to moisten, then lay over the white sugarpaste, smoothing it all over with your hands as before. Trim any excess.

Continues over the page...

5. Transfer the cake to a cake stand or plate. If you have time, allow the white layer to dry overnight at room temperature. If you don't have time, simply carry on.

6. To model the robins: use about 25g brown sugarpaste to model the first body, shaping a head, plump breast and pinching out a tail (you can mark it with a knife to look like feathers). Repeat with another 25g to make another adult bird, and then about 15g to shape the baby bird's body (B).

7. Next, use some of the red sugarpaste to make the hats. Shape 2 squat cones with about 8g sugarpaste each, hollowing out the bases a little to make space for the birds' heads. Shape on to the adult heads, adding ridges with the handle of a paintbrush to give them a more realistic appearance (C). Next, make and attach a hat for the baby bird, using about 5g red sugarpaste.

8. Using some of the white sugarpaste, make bands for the bases of the hats and stick on with a tiny bit of edible glue, if needed. Mark them with a knife, if you like, to add texture. To make the pompoms, shape small white balls and stick on to the hats, using a little edible glue if needed.

9. Using the remaining white sugarpaste, roll out thin ovals and stick to the birds' chests and sides, smoothing out the edges. Use the remaining red sugarpaste to make smaller red ovals to stick on to the centres of the white chests, again smoothing out the edges.

10. Next, shape 6 wings using the remaining brown sugarpaste; 4 larger and 2 smaller. Stick these to the sides of birds, using edible glue if needed, and mark with a knife to add a feather texture. Finally, shape tiny beaks using the orange/yellow sugarpaste and stick them to the birds' faces. Set the robins aside (leave overnight on baking paper to harden, if you have time).

11. If you like, lightly brush your holly/ivy leaves with some green lustre and roll the berries (if made) in some red lustre. Using a little edible glue to help them stick, arrange the dried leaves in a wreath around the top (and extending a little down the sides) of the cake. Next, stick on the red berries, if made.

12. Slice the Flake bars into shorter lengths and lightly dust with icing sugar to resemble snowy logs. Arrange on the cake and sit the birds on top of them. Secure a ribbon around the base of the cake, if you like, and you're good to go!

Triple-chocolate Bûche de Noël

A sure-fire winner, this crowd-pleaser always goes down a treat.

FOR THE CAKE
Butter, to grease
6 large eggs, separated
125g caster sugar
1 tsp vanilla extract
50g cocoa powder, sifted, plus extra to dust

FOR THE FILLING
200ml double cream
50g white chocolate
1 tbsp vanilla bean paste

FOR THE TOPPING
150g milk chocolate, broken into pieces
100g dark chocolate (70% cocoa solids), broken
    into pieces
150g butter, very soft
225g icing sugar, sifted
Chocolate stars and edible glitter, to decorate (optional;
    see GH TIP)

Hands-on time: 45 minutes
Cooking time: about 30 minutes
Makes 12 slices.

PER SLICE 425cals, 7g protein, 31g fat (18g saturates),
30g carbs (29g total sugars), 1g fibre

◆ TO STORE
Keep in the fridge for up to 5 days.

◆ GH TIP
We made our own chocolate stars by melting white
chocolate, pouring it into star moulds, then chilling
the stars to firm them up before drizzling with
melted dark chocolate.

1. Heat the oven to 170°C (150°C fan) mark 3.
   Grease and line the base of a 33 x 23cm Swiss
   roll tin with baking parchment. Using a handheld
   electric whisk, beat together the egg yolks and
   sugar until pale, about 5 minutes. Fold in the
   vanilla extract and cocoa powder. In a separate,
   grease-free bowl with clean beaters, whisk the
   egg whites until stiff peaks form.

2. Using a large metal spoon, gently fold a third
   of the whites into the chocolate mixture to loosen.
   Fold in the remaining whites until combined – be
   careful not to knock out too much air. Spoon into
   the prepared tin and level. Bake for 20 minutes
   until the cake feels springy to the touch.

3. Lay out a piece of baking parchment and dust
   generously with cocoa powder. Invert the cake
   on to the paper and peel away the lining paper
   from the sponge. Leave to cool on a wire rack.

4. For the filling, whisk the cream until it just holds
   its shape. Coarsely grate the white chocolate and
   fold into the cream with the vanilla bean paste.

5. To make the topping, melt the milk and dark
   chocolate in a bowl set over a pan of gently
   simmering water, making sure the bowl doesn't
   touch the water. Set aside to cool. Whisk together
   the butter and icing sugar until smooth. Fold
   through the cooled melted chocolate.

6. Spread the white chocolate filling over the cake.
   With the help of the paper, roll up the cake,
   working from a shorter side. Transfer to a plate.
   Spread over the topping and decorate with
   chocolate stars and glitter, if you like.

Index